ANTONY EASTHOPE

WHAT A MAN'S GOTTA DO

The masculine myth in popular culture

PALADIN
GRAFTON BOOKS
A Division of the Collins Publishing Group

LONDON GLASGOW
TORONTO SYDNEY AUCKLAND

Paladin
Grafton Books
A Division of the Collins Publishing Group
8 Grafton Street, London W1X 3LA

A Paladin Paperback Original 1986

Copyright © Antony Easthope 1986

ISBN 0-586-08542-4

Printed and bound in Great Britain by
Collins, Glasgow

Set in Ehrhardt

CONTENTS

PART V: MASCULINE/FEMININE

ACKNOWLEDGEMENTS

I would like to thank Rob Lapsley and Mike Westlake for criticism and ideas over a period of time that have contributed materially to all parts of this book. In addition I am grateful for discussions, containing both agreement and disagreement, with Jonathan Dollimore, Caroline Henton, Toril Moi and Alan Sinfield.

I would also like to acknowledge the help of the men and women I have worked with for some years in the area of cultural studies – Margaret Beetham, Stewart Crehan, Sue Furniss, Elspeth Graham, Alf Louvre, Tony Martin and Pam Watts. Of course what goes into a book is one thing and what comes out of it is another.

I am also grateful to the following for giving permission for the reproduction of copyright material:
the Staatliche Museum, Berlin; Galleria dell'Accademia, Florence; the Priests of the Sacred Heart, Hales Corners, Wisconsin; Biblioteca Ambrosiana, Milan; Martin Kemp and his book *Leonardo da Vinci*, published by J. M. Dent & Sons; Philip Morris Ltd; All-Sport; *Daily Mail*; Greenall Whitley Ltd; *Daily Express*; Thames Television International; *Daily Telegraph*; Associated Press; Popperfoto; Robert Graves; *The Sun*; ATV Music Ltd and Point Music Ltd; Michael Linnit Ltd; *TV Times*; Virgin Music (Publishers) Ltd; *Kiss Me Deadly* © 1953 by E. P. Dutton & Co, reprinted by permission of New English Library Ltd.

For Lilian, Carol-Ann, Diane, Annabeth,
Catherine and Kelynge

INTRODUCTION

> *So God created man in his own image,*
> *in the image of God created he him;*
> *male and female created he them.*
>
> *Genesis* 1

It is time to try to speak about masculinity, about what it is and how it works. This collection of essays looks at the images of masculinity put forward by the media today and analyses the myth of masculinity expressed through them.

Despite all that has been written over the past twenty years on femininity and feminism, masculinity has stayed pretty well concealed. This has always been its ruse in order to hold on to its power.

Masculinity tries to stay invisible by passing itself off as normal and universal. Words such as 'man' and 'mankind', used to signify the human species, treat masculinity as if it covered everyone. The God of *Genesis* is supposed to be all-powerful and present everywhere. He first makes 'man' in his own masculine image before going on to create male and female. If masculinity can present itself as normal it automatically makes the feminine seem deviant and different.

In trying to define masculinity this book has a political aim. If masculinity can be shown to have its own *particular* identity and structure then it can't any longer claim to be universal.

An ancient myth of masculinity, going back to the Greek gods of the sun, equates maleness with light. In *Genesis* there are certainly men and women but only because *he* created them. Masculinity has always tried to be present everywhere as the source of everything, and this is what makes it hard to write about. Masculinity has to be unmasked, separated from the role it wants to play by pretending to be *the* human, *the* normal, *the* social.

Two things now make it possible to define masculinity in a critical way, just as they make it politically necessary as well. The first is the revival of the women's movement since the 1960s. By the very fact of asserting the rights of women and the claims of femininity the women's movement has put masculinity in question and suggested it has its own particular identity (competitive, aggressive, violent, etc.). In the same period gay politics has openly challenged the idea of masculinity that is promoted on all sides as normal and universal.

Feminist and gay accounts have begun to make masculinity visible. But, written from a position outside and against masculinity, they too often treat masculinity as a source of oppression. Ironically, this is just how masculinity has always wanted to be treated – as the origin for everything, the light we all need to see by, the air we all have to breathe. The task of analysing masculinity and explaining how it works has been overlooked.

Popular Culture

If masculinity is not in fact universal, where is it? *The Masculine Myth* takes the version which saturates popular culture today, both British and American, in films, advertising, newspaper stories, popular songs, children's comics. This is the dominant myth of masculinity, the one inherited from the patriarchal tradition. Here it is examined in twenty-two sections. Some are long, some short, but all look at an example of how popular culture portrays men and tries to appeal to them.

Clearly these are masculine fantasies, fantasies of masculinity. When I enjoy a Robert Redford film I imagine I'm Robert Redford but I know I'm not really. Men in fact live the dominant myth of masculinity unevenly, often resisting it. But as a social force popular culture cannot be escaped. And it provides a solid base of evidence from which to discuss masculinity.

Gender can be defined in three ways: as the body; as our social roles of male and female; as the way we internalize and live out

these roles. To define masculinity in terms of the physical apparatus, the male genitals, doesn't get you very far. Sociologists
have undertaken important work on the second way of defining
masculinity, that is, in terms of male gender roles. But their writing
about male behaviour and male attitudes tends to be too descriptive.
It relies a great deal on interviews and what men are consciously
prepared to admit about themselves. Sociological work does not
look at masculinity from the inside, at the way social roles are re-
created and lived imaginatively by individuals.

When I was born I did not know whether I was going to be
Chinese, English, or Navajo Indian, but still nature had equipped
me, like everyone else, with the biological potential to live and
reproduce in any of those societies. But biology is not enough.
Every society assigns new arrivals particular roles, including gender
roles, which they have to learn. The little animal born into a
human society becomes a socialized individual in a remarkably
short time. Babies born in England go off to school five years later
to spend most of the day away from their parents. They can do
that because they have internalized and come to live for themselves
the roles of the parent society. This process of internalizing is both
conscious and unconscious. To understand it fully we need to be
able to analyse the unconscious.

Psychoanalysis and Masculinity

This book uses a psychoanalytic definition of masculinity, especially
that developed by Freud and later by the French analyst Jacques
Lacan. In 1974 Juliet Mitchell published *Psychoanalysis and Feminism,* an extraordinarily original book which did more than anything
else to revive psychoanalysis as a way of understanding gender. It
is certainly true, as Mitchell says, that 'psychoanalysis is not a
recommendation *for* a patriarchal society, but an analysis *of* one'.
Unfortunately it is also true that psychoanalysis is still in part
contaminated by the patriarchal assumptions it sets out to analyse.
Too often it regards as general something that is only or mainly
masculine. Even so, at present there is no clear alternative to
psychoanalysis for explaining the internal structures of the self –
the fantasies, wishes and drives through which we live out the
social roles of male and female. Psychoanalysis may well be

inadequate in its account of the feminine, but may still be accurate about masculinity.

A century ago Darwin discovered that the evolution of all species was determined by two needs. A species must be able to make a living by looking after itself and it must be able to reproduce itself. On this basis Freud describes the human psyche as shaped for the most part by two forms of drive. Corresponding to the instinct for self-preservation there is self-love or narcissism. Corresponding to the need to reproduce there is sexual drive. But Darwin's instincts must not be confused with Freud's drives. While instinct (*Instinkt* in German) is simply biological, a matter of genetic inheritance, drive (*Trieb*) is instinct that has been *transformed into symbolic form*. The difference is crucial but often misunderstood (and it doesn't help that the standard English translation of Freud uses 'instinct' for both terms).

The distinction means, for example, that when psychoanalysis speaks about 'the mother', it is not referring to an actual parent who nurtures you but to the mother as an idea or object that you love. This is the symbolic mother that the infant loves even if its real mother has died and her function has been taken over by an aunt or its father. Even more to the point, for psychoanalysis the penis is not the penis, a fragile and important organ of the body, like the heart or the liver. The penis is a symbolic and cultural object, the phallus. As a cultural object the phallus may attract immense force and charisma while the humble penis carries on as best it can with its usual bodily functions (it is a neatly dual-purpose organ).

There is no shortage of objections to psychoanalysis, and one of the main ones is that it ignores history. Psychoanalysis tends to regard human beings as though they are the same everywhere and always were. This is undoubtedly a valid criticism, and one which psychoanalysis should have come to terms with long ago. For it follows from the distinction between instinct and drive, between the body itself and its symbolic representation, that drive is in part culturally and historically determined.

Patriarchy is almost certainly as old as farming, the advent of which signified the replacement of collective ownership by private property. But this book does not examine the myth of masculinity anything like as far back as that. Nor does it look outside European culture. The myth certainly goes back to the ancient world of Greece and Rome; however, its present form is stamped indelibly by the Renaissance and the rise of capitalism. No attempt to analyse masculinity, even one relying on psychoanalysis, can ignore the way masculinity is defined by history.

One example would be the way gender is given a new definition by capitalism and the bourgeois culture that goes with it. From the Renaissance there has been an increasing economic split between production and consumption, between what is produced for the market and the market it is sold to. Work and leisure, the factory and the home, become widely separated. Accordingly, the idea of male and female becomes similarly separated and polarized. Work becomes masculinized while home and leisure become feminized.

Present-day car advertisements also demonstrate how ideas of gender are always historical. The ads emphasize the sleek, rounded outlines of the latest model, suggesting it has somehow made itself without human labour. And they often link this silhouette to a sharp, shiny image of a woman's body. In this way commodity fetishism and psychic fetishism are superimposed, and a particular idea of masculinity emerges: he is the master and the car is a she. So a psychoanalytic definition of masculinity cannot be timeless. It must take account of a particular culture and history.

Bisexuality

For psychoanalysis sexual identity has no core, no centre. The infant begins as a wild bundle of drives seeking pleasure without shame wherever it can be found, from the mouth, the anus, the genitals. Not yet he or she, it is 'polymorphously perverse' in Freud's phrase or, in Lacan's pun, an 'hommelette', both a 'little he-she' and, like the batter of an omelette in a pan, flowing and spreading without limit or definition. Whatever the external sexual apparatus may say, inside the infant is an active mixture of masculine and feminine, and this potential is never lost. Freud refers confidently and unequivocally to 'the constitutional bisexuality of each individual'. So everyone acquires a relatively fixed sexual identity but this sexual direction can never be more than a preference, a predominance.

The former Chinese premier Chou En Lai was once asked what he thought of the French Revolution. He replied, 'It's too soon to tell.' The same goes for psychoanalysis. I do not know whether its theories are tenable or not because it is too soon to tell and too little work has yet been done. But it does yield a systematic account of masculinity, one which doesn't just describe features but analyses them. Psychoanalysis can explain a range of different surface appearances of masculinity in terms of a single, coherent structure underlying them.

As will be seen, a number of main themes recur constantly throughout the twenty-two sections of this book. The examples of popular culture discussed are all treated from the perspective of psychoanalysis. However, the process may also work back the other way. The validity (or otherwise!) of the analysis may confirm psychoanalytic theory. Or it may not. In any case, I shall avoid technical exposition as far as possible, though for each section a list of the relevant work drawn on appears at the back.

If everyone is a mixture of masculine and feminine there is no single such thing as a male, a female, a man, a woman. *The Masculine Myth* argues that at present masculinity is defined mainly in the way an individual deals with his femininity and his desire for other men. The forms and images of contemporary popular culture lay on a man the burden of having to be one sex all the way through. So his struggle to be masculine is the struggle to cope with his own femininity. From the versions of masculinity examined here it seems that men are really more concerned about other men than about women at all. In the dominant myth it looks as though – as some feminist writing has suggested – women take on more value for men in terms of the game of masculinity than in their own right. It is for this reason that *The Masculine Myth* is divided into five parts. The first four are about masculinity trying to cope with itself and its other, feminine side. Only the final, longer section looks at men and women together.

This has been borne out by my own experience. Through no choice of my own I was born into a family in which my mother was the only woman. I went to a grammar school, which was all male, and then to university at a men's college (this has since admitted women). At work my academic department has a teaching staff of twenty-one men and seven women. This experience of living and working in a man's world is pretty typical. Since men have traditionally had the power to decide these things, it looks as though they have preferred to spend most of their time with other men rather than with women. It also looks as though this separation of home and work has been exacerbated by the development of a capitalist economy.

It is not going to be easy to write about masculinity. One difficulty is that you cannot really define masculinity apart from femininity and a male writer cannot speak for women, of what they are and what they may be. Another is that it is hard for a man to think about masculinity because at present it seems so natural, obvious and close to home. Psychoanalysis helps here since it sets masculinity at a distance and treats it as something to be understood in an objective way. To a large extent I intend to follow the logic of psychoanalysis and see where it leads. But still there is no guarantee that the writing will not warm to the theme of masculinity, endorsing it even while it is being held up for detached inspection. This book may enable others to do better.

So, trying to define masculinity is going to be a tricky and speculative venture. However, for this task psychoanalysis provides one valuable piece of extra assistance. It is an analytic, not a moralizing discourse. This is, I think, a very good thing. To be male in modern society is to benefit from being installed, willy nilly, in a position of power. No liberal moralizing or glib attitudinizing can change that reality. Social change is necessary and a precondition of such change is an attempt to *understand* masculinity, to make it visible.

The venture has one clear implication. If masculinity is not, as it claims, normal and universal but rather has a particular identity and structure, then it would be wrong to regard masculinity simply as a source, whether of oppression or anything else, as though masculinity were just there, a given. The argument will demonstrate that masculinity is an effect, and a contradictory one. In so far as men live the dominant version of masculinity analysed here, they are themselves trapped in structures that fix and limit masculine identity. They do what they *have* to do.

PART I

BASIC MASCULINITY

THE MYSTERIOUS
PHALLUS

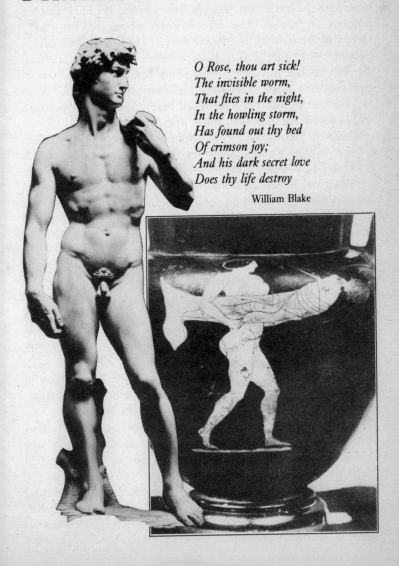

O Rose, thou art sick!
The invisible worm,
That flies in the night,
In the howling storm,
Has found out thy bed
Of crimson joy;
And his dark secret love
Does thy life destroy

William Blake

An ordinary Greek vase for storing wine or grain is decorated, as a matter of course, with an image of a naked woman marching off with something under her arm that resembles a fish or a tree-trunk but which is really a phallus. Margaret Walters in *The Nude Male* remarks of the image that 'it is not clear whether her intentions are religious or lustful'. The second image shows Michelangelo's carving of David from the biblical story of David and Goliath. It is without doubt the most famous sculpture of a male nude in the Renaissance tradition, and has inspired a whole tradition of representation of the young and athletic male body down to Tarzan and Superman. What is reproduced here comes from a postcard sold to tourists in Florence for less than 10p.

Although both images come from the main line of Western culture, a huge distance separates them. Greek society publicly celebrates male power through the symbol of the penis erect; the Christian and Renaissance world hides it away. David's right hand is larger than life but not his penis. The Greek phallus is displayed to attract women, but it is also there for men since in this society male homosexual desire is admitted explicitly. After that it goes underground and becomes sublimated into something else.

Greek Vase with Phallus

From the fifth century B.C., as Margaret Walters says, the male body becomes a normal image in art. Idealized in the form of gods – Zeus the father, Apollo the perfect son – patriarchal power is openly on view. Satyrs, often fat and hairy, are shown with huge erections; gigantic phalluses are carried at religious festivals honouring Dionysus. Instead of portrayals of the Virgin Mary or Jesus of the Sacred Heart, people put on their doorways a good-luck charm consisting of a man's head and an erect penis. This also forms the centrepiece for sculptures honouring the fertility god, Priapus. As a garden ornament he was used sometimes as a scarecrow to frighten birds. Instead of a Disney gnome ancient lawns were protected by a rigid male member. The Roman god Fascinus, represented simply as an erect penis, was carried around by people as a good-luck charm instead of a St Christopher. Images of the phallus could be seen everywhere. There was no secret about male dominance.

This is a masculinity which swings both ways. The phallus is exhibited to men and women as an object of desire. In the framework of psychoanalysis the male individual contains both a masculine aspect which desires the feminine and a feminine aspect which desires the masculine. In Greek culture masculinity is defined through both heterosexual and homosexual desire.

In a text which stands right at the beginning of the Western tradition, *The Symposium*, Plato imagines or recalls a dinner party that took place just before 400 B.C. As well as Socrates, the guests include the comic dramatist Aristophanes. It is an all-male party. Deciding not to drink too much this particular evening because they are hung-over from the night before, the men send out the last woman, a flute-girl, so that they can talk among themselves about the nature of love.

There are three main speeches. Aristophanes tells a story, that originally everyone was joined to someone else in a four-legged, two-headed body with two sets of genitals (they ran by turning cartwheels). But they got too strong for Zeus so he cut them all in half. And this is why love takes the form it does, since everyone desires his or her original partner, whether male and female, male and male or female and female.

Socrates opposes this cheerful pluralism. No women are present but nevertheless he quotes the views of a woman, Diotima, about love. Through her voice Socrates advocates the sublimation of desire – it should develop from lust for real bodies to an abstract love for 'universal beauty'. The party ends with a speech by Alcibiades, a handsome, brilliant but unreliable politician. He arrives drunk but confirms Socrates's defence of chastity because, so he says, he had tried to make love with him once, even got into bed with him, but hadn't been able to seduce him.

Perhaps it would be wrong to take Plato's work too seriously. Aristophanes is a comedian, Alcibiades is drunk. But still male homosexual desire is acknowledged as part of masculinity, not denied. Afterwards the view of Socrates wins out. As Western culture comes under the influence of Christianity the symbol of the erect penis is banished and homosexual desire is turned down other pathways.

'David' and Sublimation

Male power does not disappear along with public representations of the phallus. Far from it – patriarchy becomes more pervasive and far-reaching when it tries to be invisible. David's flaccid penis appears to be merely one part of his anatomy, carefully concealed by being in realistic proportion to the rest. But his whole body presents masculinity as though it were equivalent to confident humanity itself.

Michelangelo's naked statue shocked its contemporaries. Soon after it was set up in the town square in 1504 it was stoned one night, though it is not certain whether this was done by Michelangelo's political opponents or because the naked genitals were found so disturbing. In the period after the Council of Trent in 1563 a big effort was made to suppress nakedness in art, both male and female. There was, for example, a move to destroy Michelangelo's fresco of *The Last Judgement* on the ceiling of the Sistine Chapel in the Vatican. And a painter, Daniel da Volterra, was paid to paint over the represented genitals.

Threatened more by industrial pollution than prudery, the *David* was moved inside in 1873 to its present setting in the Accademia. Designed for the public square, its enormous height seems excessive indoors. It reproduces the Greek tradition of portraying a perfect young man. But while the Greek statues represent gods, serene and unified, appearing the same from whatever point they are viewed, David is human, mortal and contradictory. Seen from the front, with his face in profile, he is cool and relaxed. But from any other angle the twist of the neck seems strained, the frown uncertain. This ambiguity gives the figure great inwardness, an inner tension expressed across the whole of the body. His phallic potential is suggested everywhere but not explicitly stated anywhere.

The effect is partly a historical one. In the context of the biblical narrative David becomes a character in a bourgeois narrative. I Samuel 17 says that 'the king will enrich' the man who destroys Goliath, and David is the humble shepherd boy who makes good through his individual ability, in this case with a slingshot. He is also the submissive son who kills the uncircumcised Philistine and cuts off his head 'in the name of the Lord', in the name of the symbolic father. He stands for God's invisible erection.

With the suppression of public display of the phallus, masculine phallic power becomes at the time of the Renaissance an inward and spiritual force. And male homosexual desire becomes increasingly sublimated into forms of social obligation.

For psychoanalysis there is no disinterested motive, no unselfish love, nothing innate that would make us co-operate and work for the sake of others. That has to be developed. Flowing out of a single reservoir of energy, or libido, the two main drives take the form of love for oneself (narcissism) or love for another (sexual desire). This inevitably brings the individual into some conflict with social order and the law, for you either want something for yourself or desire what you can't have. Sublimation is a crucial means to resolve such conflicts.

Sexual drive can be transformed into narcissism, self-love. For example, it only takes a slight touch of 'flu for you to lose your sexual interest – the ego needs all the libido it can get and keeps it for itself. Sublimation works rather like that. If sexual drive is withdrawn into the 'I' it becomes partly desexualized and can be directed to a non-sexual end. The classic example of sublimation is art itself. The 'I' is able to tame and master sexual desire by creating or looking at pictures of desirable objects. Or someone frustrated by an unhappy sexual relationship will find an outlet by working very hard. Thus, so it's argued, sublimation is fundamental to the social order, transforming unacceptable sexual drive into something more conventional.

Clearly enough male heterosexual desire can be led to co-operate with the social order through the institution of marriage. But this does not account for the other side of masculinity, for male homosexual desire. Desexualized, sublimated love for other men becomes available to form the male bond, enabling men to work together for each other.

This is the logic behind Freud's otherwise extraordinary – and repeated – assertions that modern patriarchal society is based upon sublimated male homosexual desire. It is vividly illustrated by the Renaissance statue of David. For what is his desire? It is surely not sexual. He exercises a spiritual and inward self no Greek statue ever shows, and through this narcissistic dimension his sexual desire is transformed into social duty. He is not there for women but for himself and his father.

Michelangelo's *David* is an exceptional image of a nude male. After the Renaissance the nude is generally female, not male. And representation of the penis, whether erect or not, continues to be forbidden down to the twentieth century, as Margaret Walters recalls. In 1916 an explicitly phallic statue by Brancusi was banned from an exhibition in Paris. In 1933 a portfolio of Michelangelo's nudes was seized by customs in New York for being 'shocking pornography'. Jim Dine's exhibition of watercolours showing a variety of penises was raided and shut down by London police in 1966. In 1968 the Kronhausen's famous erotic exhibition manifested the usual inhibition about representing the phallus, even though it took place in Sweden.

On 6 June 1985 the *Guardian* newspaper reported the following incident. An artist, John Hewett, had been asked to paint 'something sporting and Grecian' for a swimming pool in the nurses' home of St Bartholomew's Hospital in London. He had done so, but after the hospital had received 'numerous complaints' the mural was covered with a heavy coat of whitewash on the orders of the hospital administrator. This was because, so he said, it had shown a 'full frontal reclining male surrounded by other naked males'. A few days later Sian Hillier SRN wrote to the paper asking whether 'young and innocent nurses' would now be issued with blindfolds for use when 'handling the unmentionable object'.

This newspaper story confirms two things about the modern myth of masculinity. One is that the phallus must remain unseen if it is to keep its power. The other is that men are more concerned about seeing 'the unmentionable object' than women.

FATHERS AND SONS

Red River, directed by Howard Hawks (1948)

In 1851, Thomas Dunson (John Wayne) leaves behind a wagon train and Fen, the woman he loves, to start up his own herd of cattle. In the distance he sees the wagons attacked by Indians and knows Fen is dead. A boy, Matthew Garth (Montgomery Clift), escapes and together he and Dunson cross the Red River. Fourteen years later, having found land, they have built up the largest herd in Texas. But after the Civil War there is no market for beef in the south so Dunson decides to drive them north to the railroad at Missouri.

At first the drive goes well. But one night there is a stampede and a man is killed. Dunson decides to whip the man responsible for frightening the cattle. The man goes for his gun and Matthew shoots him in the shoulder to prevent Dunson shooting him in the heart. Later three other men revolt against Dunson's leadership and he is forced to shoot them. Another three run off taking some food and a gunman is sent to bring them back. Meanwhile the herd crosses the Red River.

When two of the runaways are caught Dunson proposes to hang them for theft. Led by Matthew, the cowboys gang up against Dunson, take his herd and ride for Abilene (not Missouri), leaving Dunson behind. He promises to pursue them and kill Matthew. Under Matthew's leadership they rescue a wagon train from Indians and Matthew falls in love with Tess Millay. They also find the railroad and Abilene where Matthew makes a good deal to sell the cattle, keeping the money for Dunson. However, Dunson catches up with them, shoots at Matthew – who won't shoot back – until they have a fistfight. This is stopped by Tess Millay threatening them both with a gun. The men are reconciled and Dunson incorporates M for Matthew into the brand of his ranch.

*A father, said Stephen, battling against
hopelessness, is a necessary evil*

James Joyce, *Ulysses*

Where should we look for fathers and sons if not in the classic Western? *Red River* is the classic cowboy film as well, the story of the cattle drive, widely shown in the cinema at the time, now often on television. It even has a repeated song with a chorus of 'Yippee Yi Yay'. Filmed with an epic quality, especially in the crossing of the Red River, the film says something about the founding of America – indeed perhaps about capitalism itself. And the thousand-mile three-month drive suggests, albeit in a glamorized form, the nature of work in general as an active male enterprise.

The Western is a particularly masculine genre and *Red River* is an archetypal male-bond movie. Conflict between the men is acted out with a symbolic phallus – who has the fastest draw? Comedy consists of rough male banter. For example, playing poker, Groot, the garrulous old cook (Walter Brennan), loses his false teeth to an Indian in the company. When at one point on the trail he asks for them back because they 'help to keep the dust outta my mouth' Quo the Indian replies, 'Keep mouth shut. Dust not get in.' When women do appear in the film, at the beginning and the end, their performance is stilted, perhaps because they are required to act and talk more like men than women. Women are kept to the margins in *Red River*, even though in the end they are what is at stake, what is fought for.

Male Sexual Identity

There is a story that George Washington never wanted to found the United States. All he wanted was a commission in the British Army but when this was refused he said, 'OK, I'll get my own damn country and my own damn army.' Psychoanalysis understands the construction of male sexual identity along rather similar lines. The male infant, like every infant, actively seeks to keep the mother and her love for himself. To become a heterosexual man the little boy must transfer his love from the mother to another adult woman, a figure that for convenience – and with no necessary commitment to the institution of marriage – may be termed 'the bride'. To become a heterosexual woman the little girl must transfer her love from the mother *to the father* and then to the figure of the bridegroom. The path to adult, heterosexual identity is not symmetrical but both sexes begin by actively seeking the mother. Both must give up the mother from fear of castration.

All this is a symbolic process. No act of castration is literally carried out – it's a matter of drive, not instinct. It would solve a lot of problems if psychoanalysis could simply describe castration as the loss of the mother, as lack. However, this loss is symbolized by the idea of loss of the genitals, the worst thing in the world. It is worse than death, says Freud, because fear of death is only a shadow of this. In wanting the mother the little boy comes into competition with the father and feels threatened with castration. Because of this he surrenders one object, the mother, and comes to desire another, the bride. In so doing he is able to identify with the father and prepare to take his own place as a father.

This is the ideal model but it hardly ever works out like that. On the path to adult heterosexual desire the little boy has to find a way between two dangers. If he has been too submissive to the father he must challenge him for the mother's love, otherwise he'll never come to take the role of the father. On the other hand, if he attacks the father too much and refuses to accept castration, he remains rebellious and infantile, unable to give up his attachment to the mother. The two possibilities correspond to the two sides of the little boy's sexuality, or rather bisexuality. His heterosexual side seeks the mother and opposes the father. But his homosexual side tries to avoid the father's threat by taking the mother's place and becoming the object of the father's love.

It is exactly this divided sexuality that the myth of masculinity wants to deny. Although men are always both masculine and feminine, the myth demands that they should be masculine all the way through.

Fathers and Sons in 'Red River'

So to Thomas Dunson (John Wayne) in this classic Western. It is striking that this symbolic father manages to get a son without depending at all on the other sex. The woman he was going to marry is killed and he finds the snake-bracelet he gave her on a dead Indian. A boy, a survivor of the massacre, turns up and Dunson gives him the bracelet. Matthew is his symbolic son, one he has produced completely in his own image, like God siring Jesus. Here we come across a deep and ancient foundation of the masculine myth. It is at the heart of the Christian tradition. And the idea that fathers make sons out of themselves and not by sexual union is repeated all the time in such everyday phrases as 'a chip off the old block' or 'a spitting image'.

The John Wayne figure, like God the Father, embodies the fantasy of a man who makes himself out of nothing and who is therefore purely masculine, a hard man all through. In *Red River* Dunson has no parents. He has a son but no wife. Crossing the Red River into Texas he says 'it's everything a man could want' and it will be 'mine'. When a Mexican claims the land Dunson shoots him and reads the Bible over his grave. He is both judge and jury, teacher and preacher. With all the ruthless determination of the masculine ego he gets his men to drive the cattle north, giving them no rest. The cowboys are his sons. One he tries to whip for stealing sugar – 'only a kid steals sugar'. Another three rebel against him and he shoots them. When he decides to hang the two who steal food, one complains that the law might see it differently. Dunson replies, 'I'm the law.' He is projected as the full father, wholly self-sufficient masculine will.

All of this gives Matthew the son little room for manoeuvre. At first he submits entirely and takes up a feminine position towards the father. He wears the snake-bracelet destined for Dunson's bride and constantly lights Dunson's cigarettes for him or passes him one already lighted. When at one point Matthew says the men have 'had a really tough day, I think . . .', Dunson interrupts him with, 'I'll do the thinking, move 'em on'. The relation is signalled very much in the look of the two actors. Wayne's masculinity, his rocky face, awkward build, resonant voice and sardonic smile, are matched with Montgomery Clift's femininity, his arched dark eyebrows, wide eyes, long eyelashes, delicate nose, thin body.

Father threatens son but son also threatens father. Dunson's enclosed sufficiency begins to weaken – he can't sleep, starts drinking, gets wounded in the leg, begins to look awful. And

Matthew's masculine side begins to win out over his feminine love for the father. Although he helped Dunson do it, he says he was wrong to shoot the three rebels. Finally, when Dunson tells the two thieves who've been captured 'I'm going to hang you', Matthew interjects, 'No you're not.' And he leads the men as they gang together to overthrow Dunson and take away his cattle.

It is a moment like this that Freud imagines in his parable of the origin of patriarchy in *Totem and Taboo*. There the first father had all the women for himself until the sons combine to kill him, eat him, and get the women for themselves. Of course they suffer terrible guilt. So do the cowboys under Matthew's more gentle command. Dunson's parting words are, 'I'll kill you. Every time you turn round expect to see me.' His spectre haunts them. They are constantly jumping at shadows, pulling guns on each other, having nightmares.

However, the challenge to the father gains Matthew the bride. Turning aside with the cattle from the drive north they find a wagon train with 'women and coffee', as it's reported. Matthew meets Tess Millay, loves her, gives her the snake-bracelet. In a strange scene when Dunson later meets Tess he notices the bracelet and offers her half his property if she'll bear him sons. This full father wants everything for himself, including all the women. The endless conflict between father and son reaches its climax when they fight at the end. Matthew has sold the cattle in the name of the father and has won the bride. This is with his masculine side. But with his feminine side he stands mute, a passively suffering Jesus, and won't shoot back at Dunson when Dunson fires at him. They fight with fists until Tess Millay, acting for society and law, threatens to kill them both if they won't stop. Dunson tells Matthew to marry Tess and at last gives his symbolic son social recognition by including his initial in the emblem of the ranch.

Although the film puts the game of masculinity at the centre of attention, the feminine is what is at stake. It only appears, though, in various ways in a disguised and subordinated form. There is continual conflict between father and son, and also between the sons – Matthew has Cherry Vallance (John Ireland) as his rival for the fastest draw. The mother is the implicit object of this conflict and rivalry, symbolized in the love-token, the snake-bracelet. The feminine is what their masculine will aims to master, surrounding them in the form of the beauty of the landscape they pass through, the Red River itself which they must cross, the cattle on whom the cowboys lavish all their concern as they gently herd them north. The feminine, one might say, is the hidden object of their drive. And femininity is present throughout in their own divided sexuality.

Referring to Dunson Tess Millay says to Matthew, 'You love him, don't you? And he must love you.' Around the father/son relation *Red River* shows some essential features of the male bond and a patriarchal social order based on sublimated male homosexual desire. In fact the film examines two possible organizations of the male bond.

One is based on Dunson as patriarch. As the self-sufficient father he demands that the sons all be equally self-reliant. He makes the cowboys sign up individually before the drive and reminds the quitters, before shooting them, that they freely chose to come along: 'I'm going to have to hold you to it.' Dunson's society is based on fear and love for the father. This changes when Matthew Garth takes over – he is always been spoken of in the movie as 'too soft'. His society is organized much more in terms of love between brothers and mutual sublimated desire. It is even suggested that the difference corresponds to one between capitalism and some kind of common ownership. Dunson's rule is identified with private property – it is his land, his herd, his brand on the cattle. The men sell their labour to him and when they desert him he buys others. In contrast, when the ranch-hands take over the herd one of them tells Dunson, 'this herd don't belong to you. It belongs to every poor hoping and praying cattleman in the whole wide state.' Matthew's leadership complies with a more democratic way of making decisions, as, for example, when they turn aside to rescue the wagon train. But the price of the steers is returned to Dunson at the end when Matthew earns his place as the rightful son.

Red River perfectly illustrates a main feature of the masculine myth, a social order relying on the endless negotiation of conflict. An effective compromise can almost always be reached, for two reasons, one masculine, one feminine. On behalf of their masculine side the cowboys attack the father, though their rebellion cannot go on for ever since its object is the mother. Behind the figure of Dunson stands the law, not just its present embodiment as the capitalist law over private property, but the law of all human society which forbids the child to possess the mother if he or she wants to grow up. On behalf of their feminine side the cowboys share in the male bond. In terms of his masculinity, Matthew fights the father; in terms of his femininity he loves him and submits to him. Similarly the cowboys live in the companionship of sublimated homosexual desire, part war, part love affair. Unless defused through banter, argument is always likely to break into open conflict. At the same time the men want to resolve antagonism because they love each other and have a motive for acting unselfishly towards each other. During the stampede one falls off his horse. At risk to themselves two men ride into the seething mass of horns, lift the fallen comrade by both arms, and carry him to safety.

Jesus the Obedient Son

This religious image (see p. 24) was printed in Italy, copyrighted in the United States and bought in a newsagent's in Britain. What is so particularly unsettling about it is the real/surreal juxtaposition of an almost photographically realistic image of a man's head and shoulders with an elaborately symbolic sacred heart. The allegory is complex but represents Christ's willingness to submit to crucifixion. The heart symbolizes the body on the cross with a cut on its right side and two drops of blood representing the left side pierced by the soldier's spear. The thorns round it are the crown of thorns forced on to Christ's brow before the crucifixion. The fire surmounted by another cross represents his burning love and his passion or suffering for mankind. In the fifth symbolic image, the light shining from behind the heart recalls that Christ is the light of the world. There is a tension represented twice – between Christ's burning love symbolized by the heart and the fire and its consequence in suffering symbolized by the thorns and the cross. Heart and flame are images with obvious enough sexual connotations (an old lover is 'an old flame').

The heart, shaped and coloured like a ripe strawberry, is an

image with disconcertingly feminine associations. But then so is the whole portrayal of Christ's face. Every feature is feminized. The hair is long and wavy, parted in the middle and curling at the ends; the skin is perfectly smooth and in the colour original exudes a soft, pink glow; it is a straight little nose and a small pursed mouth.

Moustache and beard are as soft, fine and mutedly masculine as they could be. But the eyes, the main feature, are enormous – huge almond eyes with a touch of mascara, long sweeping lashes, thin pencilled brows. Since the head is bent slightly forward and to its right, the look comes out to us from under the lids, and that is a look much more often associated with pictures and photographs of women. The attraction and undoubted power of the image comes from the tension it exhibits. Careful realism is forced alongside Baroque symbolism, love and suffering cancel each other out, the masculine identity of the figure contains an intense feminization of all its details. Only the enormously powerful institution of organized Christianity could legitimate such an unusual picture, turn it into an image to be taken with profound seriousness and reverence.

Its meaning is not difficult to determine. In *Red River* the son moves from submission to the father into an attack upon him. Jesus is the son who remains entirely subservient to the father and who accordingly shows only his femininity. Jesus does not marry and his interest in women in the New Testament is not sexual. In many ways he seems more interested in and closer to men, his disciples. Instead of challenging the father for the bride he passively endures the father's aggression and is penetrated by thorns and nails. 'Father . . . not my will, but thine, be done', *Luke* 22, 42. Jesus's passivity follows from the absence of the mother, the vacuum left by Mrs God. The Christian Father has no wife and therefore Jesus has no object to desire and to contest with the father. This is the most powerful myth in the whole Western tradition. Its version of masculinity celebrates the son's feminine love for his father and complete obedience to him.

The sacrifice of Christ is anticipated in the Old Testament story of Abraham and Isaac. A few years ago the Open University started a course on European drama. It was accompanied by televised productions of plays on the syllabus, including *The Balcony* by Genet. Because this was scheduled to go out at 11 A.M. on Sunday morning, and because it had some footage of bosoms and bottoms, a Christian organization was able to get the BBC to ban it. Considered fit for Sunday viewing, the rest were transmitted as usual, including a medieval play about Abraham and Isaac. I was watching this when my youngest child, then a boy of three, came into the room and asked what it was. One is supposed to answer children's questions honestly so I said it was about a father who was going up a mountain with his son.

'Why?' he asked.

'Because when they get to the top he's going to kill him,' I said.

'Why?' he asked, looking horrified.

'Because God told him to.' At this he left the room and has not felt the same about God ever since.

Boys Will Be Boys

'Dennis the Menace and Gnasher' from *The Beano*, 8 September 1984

For a Junior Showtime in a public hall Dennis and his mates practise on their guitars. They play so loudly that they frighten the 'softies', Walter and his pals, but end up by breaking their own guitars. Their place in the show is taken by the softies and Walter's String Quartet. On stage the softies play on two violins, a cello and a harp. Seeing this Dennis says, 'ARGH! HOW GHASTLY!' and he and Gnasher whirl lassos, capturing the four softies. When the curtain goes up the softies are dancing on the stage like puppets, the lassos having become strings that Dennis and his mates pull. 'THEY'RE A "STRING QUARTET" NOW ALL RIGHT!', says Dennis.

But the announcer tells the audience that the next turn is a 'NOT SO JUNIOR POP GROUP!'. And the last frame shows Dennis's father and the other dads angrily coming on stage with slippers to beat the boys. 'THAT'S SHOWBUSINESS', says Dennis, clinging to his comrades, while the audience leap to their feet shouting, 'THIS'LL BE GOOD!'

What are little boys made of?
Slugs and snails and puppy dogs' tails,
That's what little boys are made of

The Beano is the most famous children's comic in Britain. Selling at 16p, untold thousands are bought every Thursday by boys and sometimes by girls between the ages of seven and eleven. It contains about twelve separate narratives, each on a separate page, each with its own regular character, including 'Roger the Dodger', 'Minnie the Minx', 'Lord Snooty', 'Biffo the Bear' and 'The Bash

Street Kids'. Most popular at present, 'Dennis the Menace and Gnasher' (Gnasher is his dog) appears in colour on the front and back cover. Drawn always in a simple uncluttered style with clear primary colours, the images are like the famous saucy seaside postcards of Donald McGill.

Both images and setting are attractively stylized and old-fashioned. For example, Dennis's dad is bald and has a little Hitler moustache; he always wears a trilby hat with a black band, a tie and a baggy striped suit that comes from the early 'fifties, if not the 'thirties. Like a cinema cartoon the story works very much at the level of fantasy, especially fantasies of omnipotence. In the example, one could ask where Dennis gets his cowboy lassos from, let alone the skill to land them right on target on the softies? And puppet strings could not possibly lift people off the ground. A desire for omnipotence is related to the idea of a scheme or project, which is very important in 'Dennis' and the other *Beano* stories. Fantasy or wish-fulfilment suits well with the vivid and witty style of drawing, the broad puns and direct address to the reader. Walter, for instance, is often introduced by an arrow and the words 'WALTER VERY SOFT BOY'.

There is a lot of repetition in the narratives and one suspects that they are recycled every year with the references updated. A typical narrative shows Dennis and Gnasher undertaking some scheme, either to help someone or to hinder – menace – them. The scheme has unforeseen consequences, sometimes pleasurable but more often leading to punishment, as in the example. Dennis's story very often ends with him being beaten by his father, sometimes his granny, though the act of beating is not seen.

This story ends with a beating literally staged, both for the fictional audience and for the comic's readers.

Dennis and Walter

Dennis the Menace and Walter the softy are complementary opposites, a couple. They live next door to each other, sometimes play together, constantly interact, usually when Dennis menaces Walter by putting ice down the back of his jumper or shooting at him with his pea-shooter. Although close they don't seem to go to the same school. Walter is clearly marked as middle-class, while

Dennis is working-class – though his father goes to work in a suit, carrying a briefcase.

Menaces and softies, Dennis and Walter, imply each other and are defined against each other. Walter has brushed hair and wears glasses. Dennis's mop stands up in phallic spikes. Dennis wears a hooped red and black football jersey with red and black football socks; Walter wears a blue jumper and a black and white spotted bow tie. Walter's friends have names like 'Bertie Blenkinsop' while Dennis's are called 'Curly' and 'Pie Face'. Dennis and his friends actively invent schemes; Walter and the softies play nursery rhyme games. Dennis hates school and tries to get out of it; Walter passes exams. Dennis plays pop music very loudly on guitars; Walter, as in the extract, plays the violin in a string quartet. In other stories he plays the piano.

The pairing of Walter and Dennis gives the dominant codes of what is masculine and what effeminate for a wide range of male behaviour. In one narrative Walter gets a job as the speaking clock because of his 'pleasant voice' and middle-class accent – Dennis is dismissed because he is too 'gravelly-voiced'. Dennis is physically strong, Walter is weak, and in one episode Dennis mixes concrete while Walter mixes a cake. In the winter Walter wears a blue duffle-coat and is afraid of catching cold. Dennis wears only a scarf. When on one occasion they both eat curries, Walter steams and sweats over 'A VERY MILD CURRY' while Dennis enjoys 'A HOT VINDALOO CURRY', as the arrowed messages point out.

However, Walter has a number of attributes Dennis doesn't, and does various things he doesn't. Walter gives gifts of flowers and perfume to women. He faints and swoons. When frightened he squeals and the balloon says 'SQUEAL'. When triumphant over Dennis, which does happen, he cries, 'NA NA NANA NA'. He gardens, is kind to animals, especially cats, and in one story carefully puts doll's boots on 'Poor Fluffy' because 'her little paws are cold with all this nasty snow'. She is then chased by Gnasher but finds the boots useful for stopping on the ice while Gnasher skids head-first into a snowman. Walter is carefully obedient to parents and tells tales on Dennis ('SIR! SIR! DENNIS HAS BEEN HORRID').

The crucial difference between Dennis and Walter lies in their relations to their family. Dennis is in competition with his father and calls him 'DAD'. In return he is spoken of as 'LAD' or 'MY BOY'. Walter calls his father 'DADDYKINS', even on occasion 'MY DADDYKINS', terms which suit his father who at bedtime sings to his son, 'Diddle-Diddle Dumpling, My son John ...' Walter is as close to his mother as to his father, brings her tea, calls her 'MUMSIE'. Dennis calls his mother 'MUM', won't help unless he's forced to and rejects vehemently the idea of intimacy with her. In one episode, scared by a horror film on television, she clutches Dennis and Gnasher. He turns to the reader and says 'IMAGINE MENACES GETTING CUDDLED'.

'Mum' versus 'Mumsie', Gnasher versus Foo-Foo

Dennis then is the masculine side of a boy, the side which challenges law and the father but accepts symbolic castration, imaged as beating on the buttocks. Walter represents the feminine side which loves the father and submits to him. Walter will remain childish, outside conflict with the father. Dennis, in contrast, identifies with the father since in accepting punishment he agrees that the father is right. So it is in the example above, for he submits to his beating with, 'AH WELL ... THAT'S SHOWBUSINESS'. Dennis is well set on the path that will lead him from being a 'menace' to being a hard man. Week after week the narratives act out the same fantasy for their readers – that the mother must be surrendered ('IMAGINE MENACES GETTING CUDDLED') and that masculine identity depends on expelling every touch of femininity. The two don't necessarily go together though they are inextricably joined in 'Dennis the Menace' and elsewhere in the dominant culture.

Since he has not challenged the father for possession of the mother, Walter stays childish. He is not so much feminine as polymorphous and infantile. While his identity is passive and fluid, Dennis is active and specific in his aims. The contrast comes out strongly in the two versions of their other selves represented by their dogs. Walter's pet is a toy poodle called 'Foo Foo', while Dennis has Gnasher. Gnasher is a mongrel whose hair sticks up like his master's. He is all head and teeth, teeth which can function on occasion as a circular saw. Constantly hungry, he chases cats on sight. Clearly Gnasher is the phallus, though a suitably boyish phallus. His appetitiveness is a genital form (chasing pussies) disguised as the oral (he eats anything).

Because he has won his own identity, Dennis exhibits an unformed masculine ego (discussed further in the next section). He is uncontrollably active – for instance, when he comes into the room he throws open the door and knocks his mother to the ground. Through his schemes he seeks to master the world. He tries landscape gardening in one story and while Gnasher digs holes, Dennis makes a river with the garden hose. Menaced by Minnie the Minx he turns a tree into a catapult to throw mud at her, is chased by his father, dives into one of Gnasher's tunnels and comes up in the softies' garden. Dennis lives in fantasies of the omnipotence of his will – sometimes people run away at the sight of this menace. His schemes always come unstuck because they are unrealistic. And although the usual outcome is a slippering or other threatened punishment, there is another possible consequence. He may return to the world of the softies, coming up in their garden or getting perfume and flowers dumped on him.

The two forms of punishment suggest very well the structure of the version of masculinity on offer. The necessary task of growing up is tangled up with an unnecessary denial of the feminine. Dennis's schemes are unrealistic because their hidden object is the mother. They contain an incestuous desire for an impossible world and that is why he is beaten for them. But this inevitable surrender of the mother and childishness is linked to an expulsion of the femininity from his nature. That is why his schemes are so often directed against Walter, why he can never seem to escape Walter, and why a return to femininity – if he comes up in Walter's garden – is meant to count as a punishment.

Dennis is close to home, both because the strip is comic and because it shows the very act of the construction of masculinity. It is hard to write about Dennis without affection. Nevertheless, seen at a critical distance, it is clear that in moving towards adult identity Dennis does not simply achieve a predominance of the masculine. He tries to be exclusively and only masculine, a menace, a hard man all through. With him the boyish imagination is trapped by a limiting both/and. Dennis must reject both the mother and the femininity in himself. They are only run together in this dominant version of masculinity. Mumsie does have to go but Foo Foo doesn't.

The feminine in male nature can never be suppressed. Both Dennis and Walter are staged for the reader of *The Beano*, quite literally in my example, for the audience shout 'THIS'LL BE GOOD' and we watch with them. Dennis is an ideal self the reader officially imagines he identifies with, but he must also secretly identify with Walter. Besides being extravagantly pleasurable in himself (who else but Walter would put doll's boots on 'Poor Fluffy' in the snow?), Walter is a built-in necessity without which the fun can't happen. His femininity is the cause of the narrative which the reader enjoys.

PART II

THE MASCULINE EGO

The Castle of the Self

I think therefore I am

René Descartes

Found in a discarded family album in a junk shop, this snapshot shows two boys playing at sandcastles. Most home photography consists of shots of the family, mostly on holiday, very often at the seaside. Instant memory, a tenth of a second frozen from the process of time, the image gains immediate pathos because it is so recognizably human, because it is irredeemably lost for ever. One boy stands and smiles confidently at us over his handiwork, the other is kneeling anxiously to watch the sea's attack. That gesture, that precise pose, is as temporary as the castle of sand undermined by the tide. The clothes suggest the late 'forties, with a tie (still knotted) and those long, baggy shorts. Even the sleeveless pullover adds meaning: this is an English summer. As always in a snapshot other incidental figures in the background go on with their own unrelated activities – a woman carries a child and in the distance two bathers try out the chilly water. But the centre of interest is the castle and its artificers. For the castle is designed both to withstand the sea and be destroyed by it, and pleasure attaches both to building it and watching its erosion. One boy smiles, the other frowns, just like the two sides of Michelangelo's *David*.

Even this sandcastle has a history, unlike those Chinese boys might build to repel the Pacific. This is a medieval European castle with a keep connected to an inner wall and surrounded by an outer rampart. A gap admits water to form a moat, temporarily increasing the strength of the defences until the sea, the enemy within, betrays the whole structure and only the seagull's feather from the top is left floating on the rising tide. In the boys' game the sole function of the castle is to defend itself.

Psychoanalysis claims that when the image of a building appears in dreams it usually symbolizes the self and the dreamer's own identity. But there are different kinds of buildings.

Of course every individual, to count as a human individual, must have a sense of their own identity, a sense of 'me' as opposed to everything that is other than me. Anthropology confirms that every known human society operates with a system of naming that designates a single person, however much that name links the bearer to others in their family, tribe or clan. And every human language has a means to signify the equivalent of 'me' and 'I', though again the grammar of the first-person singular varies widely from one society to another. Whereas the European languages constantly invoke the first person as a point of origin for ideas and beliefs ('I think he is . . .', 'I wonder if you . . .'), Chinese, for example, apparently only specifies 'I' when it is important that the speaker is doing something rather than someone else. So the ego, to use the terms of psychoanalysis, is a necessary human attribute but one whose particular form and weight differ greatly in different cultures and periods of history.

And so it may be with the gender of the ego. Published in 1927,

Virginia Woolf's novel *To the Lighthouse* is a deeply thoughtful and perhaps prophetic analysis of what it means to be a woman. In the second section, 'Time Passes', nothing happens; or rather what happens is that over a decade a large seaside house, neglected by its owners, slowly becomes more dilapidated as nature and weather work on it. Plaster falls from the ceiling; swallows nest in the drawing-room. There is a boundary between outside and inside but it is one which is constantly crossed and which does not hope to close its frontier completely. If this house presents a version of the feminine ego, then in the dominant myth the masculine ego is generally imaged as a military fortification, especially in the last four hundred years of Western culture.

Da Vinci's Castle
Leonardo da Vinci, Renaissance man, was a scientist as well as an artist. As part of his science he drew maps, made plans for water-works both for irrigation and transport and designed machinery to dig and move earth. He also worked as a military engineer, a job for which there was plenty of call during the endless warring between the Italian city-states of the Renaissance. During his early fifties, from 1502–3, he was employed by Cesare Borgia to design fortifications for the war between Florence and Pisa. Jacopo IV Appiani, the Pope's son, ruler of Piombino on the west coast south of Livorno, had been ousted in 1501 by Cesare Borgia, but by 1504 the situation had changed, and Florence started to support him. Someone in Florence, probably Da Vinci's acquaintance Machiavelli, had the idea of sending him to Piombino to work as a military adviser for Jacopo. In November 1504 he seems to have designed for Piombino the most brilliant and modern of his many plans for a fortified citadel (see p. 38).

This leaf from Da Vinci's notebooks is hard to disentangle and his left-handed mirror-writing doesn't help. At the top is a cutaway side-drawing of the castle; underneath a detail of the top of the parapet; and to its right a plan drawing of the whole circle to show the lines of fire. To make it clearer a modern reconstruction from the designs is included, though unfortunately this leaves out a central pillar which seems to function as a watch-tower. Other details are sketched in the margins.

Leonardo da Vinci, *Designs for a Castle* (1504)

Modern reconstruction of the castle

His design looks more like defences from 1914–18 than from the first years of the sixteenth century. Circular, it consists of three fortified rings arranged inside each other, each to be built from massive masonry, surrounded by floodable moats and protected on the outside by four outlying bastions. Whereas previous fortifications had bastions and towers that presented a vertical surface to cannon balls, this offers a series of rising contours intended to deflect them so that they bounce off according to the laws of reflected motion, as Da Vinci's notes make clear. But the danger of a fortified building is that parts of it can be used by an attacker if they are taken. Da Vinci's rings are connected by wooden bridges that can be burned once the defenders have run to inner safety across them. In addition the rings are connected by underground passages, and he has also invented a hydraulic system by which, he says, he can flood the moats and 'all the subterranean passages individually or all at once'. And further, the inner side of each ring has large openings so that if the enemy takes them they cannot hide in them.

Vision, sight and surveillance is integral to the whole design. In *Discipline and Punish*, his book on the design of prisons in the early nineteenth century and the system of power they embody, Michel Foucault draws attention to Jeremy Bentham's design for a Panopticon. This was a circular arrangement of cells that allowed every prisoner to be watched all the time from one central point. Da Vinci was there nearly three centuries before. From its centre 'one single guard watches the whole castle both inside and outside without moving'. But this is not only for defence against the enemy without – it's also a precaution against a possible enemy within. He claims that the commander 'can always hear and see the conversations and movements of his garrison without being seen'. Thus the commander 'cannot be taken by treason of his own garrison'.

Freud wrote a book on Da Vinci in which he attempted to give a psychoanalytic explanation of his career and his shifts between art and science. His two areas of interest correspond roughly to the two main forms of drive, self-love or narcissism and sexual drive, which in Da Vinci's case showed a mainly homosexual preference. Since art is a form of sublimated desire, Freud regards Da Vinci's paintings of beautiful young men and limpid Madonnas as expressions of his sexual drive. But the scientific projects, the attempts to master nature through knowledge, are explained in terms of narcissism and the ego. Turning back from sexuality in middle age Da Vinci 'became an investigator' instead of an artist and spent his time drawing up schemes, like that for Piombino.

The design for the fortress provides a masculine narcissistic fantasy and is in many ways a model of the masculine ego itself. The castle is both stake and agent in a ceaseless struggle to keep itself together, to close all gaps, watch every move, meet aggression with aggression. The purpose of the masculine ego, like that of the castle, is to *master* every threat, and here the male term is particularly appropriate. The castle of the ego is defined by its perimeter and the line drawn between what is inside and what outside. To maintain its identity it must not only repel external attack but also suppress treason within. It will not be surprising in terms of the argument of this book if the enemy within the masculine individual turns out to be his own femininity.

There is one other point. The castle of the ego depends on what is other than itself, not vice versa. Although the castle meets attacks, its only aim is to do that, so it is in the end defined by what attacks it. The two boys would have been very disappointed if the tide had turned and the sea never reached their sandcastle.

Piombino was never built. Yet Da Vinci's plan, drawn up so early in the bourgeois period, continues to give the dominant culture a fantasy of the masculine ego. It is reproduced in every scheme for impregnable defence from boys' comics to Ronald Reagan's 'Star Wars' system.

Aggression and the Masculine Ego

The ego is not born in you but has to be developed. At first the infant cannot distinguish between itself and the outside world. Its 'I' is brought into existence as it comes to identify itself as inside and everything else as outside, the self being defined by what is other than the self. The ego has no energy or libido of its own and so must draw it from its reservoir in the unconscious, the id. It is able to do this because the id comes to feel loss, especially loss of the breast and the mother. It is as though the ego says to the id, 'Look, you can love me instead of what you've lost'. To maintain and defend itself and the line between inside and outside the 'I' has two strategies, disavowal and denial. Through disavowal (*Verleugnung*) it can deal with something in the outside world by pretending it doesn't exist; and through denial (*Verneinung*) it can cope with threats from the inner world, particularly from the unconscious, by trying to keep them repressed.

This all takes continual effort. The house must always be kept up – rain gets in through the roof where a tile has come off, some wallpaper lifts off in the living-room. The castle must be constantly defended against hostile troops and treacherous members of the garrison. The human ego identifies its unity above all in an image of the body as a unified whole and fears above all the image of the body in pieces. But it goes deeper than that, for the two images depend on each other. Since the ego was never there in the first place, it has been organized out of fragments bound together by force to make up a unity. The energy that binds it is always likely to be released against anything that tends to pull it to pieces again. That is why for psychoanalysis aggression is an effect of the ego and the ego's struggle to maintain itself.

If this idea seems unlikely, we might think of the pleasure to be derived from some examples of popular culture that are otherwise hard to explain. In children's film cartoons the body is continually burned, squashed, smashed, dropped from a great height, and blown up. Yet it always magically reconstitutes itself in its original form for the next sequence. Tom gets run over by a steamroller, flattened to paper, peels himself off the ground and then races off after Jerry as though nothing had happened. Then he runs into a tree and the process is repeated.

Another two examples relate to the way in which television channels and individual programmes identify themselves. Both reassure the viewer by demonstrating that what comes to pieces fits back together again. One is the logo for Channel 4, a figure 4. In one version of the station signal the 4 dissolves into dozens of tiny pieces and then is remade from the other side by as many fragments. At the same time the tones rise and fall, returning to almost the same note as the one on which they started (or so my younger daughter says). In another version the 4 is broken into nine pieces, two each of yellow, blue, green and purple, and one red bit. These sail into the centre to make up a coherent 4, with the joins still showing as in a jigsaw or child's toy.

The Independent Television lunch-time news has a complex, 30-second-long title sequence, beginning with the ITN logo and the sound of Big Ben striking one. Part of the sequence shows a flat outline of the world which folds round to make a globe. This starts to spin from east to west as the earth does and the viewer is positioned to see it from a satellite above it (we are 'the eye of the sun'). As it spins, chunks of territory lift up from the globe towards the viewer – South America, North America, the Soviet Union,

China, the Middle East – and then fall snugly back into place again. Only Europe and finally the United Kingdom stay immune to dislocation, remaining fixed as the viewpoint of the camera sweeps low over them. Here the sequence cuts to the newsreader at his desk and the written words NEWS AT ONE. 'One' has the double meaning of one o'clock and of the earth itself whose pieces make up a satisfying unity, a world 'at one'. (The titles also link the phallic figure of Big Ben and his number one, a male newsreader, and a map of the United Kingdom, an association that will be taken up in terms of 'Man and Nation'.)

As these examples suggest, the identity of the ego is not only secured in space but also in time. Parts are actively bound into a provisional unity but equally a process is fixed into some kind of permanence. The 'I' must persist as a continuing identity. The one true generalization is that time makes everything always different, alters it, however slightly. Against this the ego must maintain that it is always the same. In the middle of change it must find repetition and establish itself as a fixture. Both binding (in space) and fixing (in time) are active forms of defence and denial: I don't mean that, I don't come to pieces, I don't change. The force so bound is all the more likely to explode into aggression against what is other than the self. And this is the case for everyone.

To describe the binding of energy, psychoanalysis generally makes use of three kinds of metaphor: hydraulics and the flow of water giving the idea of pressure, electricity that of charge, capitalism that of investment. Using these we can say that there must be distinctions between the *amount* of pressure, charge or investment needed to synthesize the ego. It will depend how tightly the pieces are tied together, how firm the fixture tries to be, how harshly a line is to be held between inside and out, whether for the house or the castle.

At present in the dominant myth the masculine ego is imagined as closing itself off completely, maintaining total defence. To be unified it must be masculine all the way through and so the feminine will always appear as something other or different and so a security risk. When it is in the external world outside the self the feminine will be a lovely enemy for whom desire triumphs over narcissistic anxiety. But when the feminine seems to have infiltrated within, as it must do because of the bisexual nature of every individual, it threatens the whole castle and must be savagely suppressed. Either way, since defence is attack, the more the 'I' strives to be total master, the more aggression it releases.

Defensive mastery requires constant vigilance. The masculine ego must be watchful and it will also be anxious, and these effects are worked out very much in terms of sight and vision. In the seaside photograph the confident smile of one boy is answered by the watchful frown of the other. And Da Vinci's fort is designed to be under continuous and total surveillance: 'one single guard watches the whole castle both inside and outside without moving'. The centre, the eye at the middle of the 'I', can seem to be an ideal point above and beyond the system it watches over, though of course it isn't – if Da Vinci's castle falls, so will the central watch-tower. But film and television can give the impression that the eye of the 'I' is outside it. We are invited to watch the Channel 4 logo form and re-form from a position of safety outside the process. And so also with the titles for 'News at One'. The camera places the viewer above and beyond the world's disturbing coming apart and going back together again. This kind of visual dominance, seeing and knowing everything, comes from a particularly masculine perspective, as will be discussed later. To keep in sight means to keep under control.

The theme of mastery and the masculine ego will recur in the sections that follow; for example, in relation to the body, and also to the idea of the nation. It is hard to draw a firm line between the ego's necessary self-love which watches out for real dangers and the obsessive and anxious watchfulness of the masculine ego. This goes well beyond realistic assessment of risk into an attempt to master all possible dangers by thinking about them in advance, as though the power of thought itself could ward them off. For the masculine ego this leads to a brutal insistence on what can happen and aggressive denial of what you would like to happen. (In its portrait of Mr Ramsay, the novel *To the Lighthouse* demonstrates this very well.) But over-insistence on harsh realism will manifest itself everywhere, for example in the section on banter as a masculine style.

Watching out for attack is hard to distinguish from excessive fear of fancied attack from outside, and that is, quite simply, paranoia. The defensiveness of the masculine ego means that it always falls under the shadow of paranoia, and this we will return to later on in connection with the fear of homosexuality (homophobia) and also with jealousy. But mention of paranoia, of the watchfulness of the would-be masterful ego, is a good way to recall just what the ego wishes to deny and forget: that it depends on a process outside itself for its very existence. That in the end is the threat it exists to counter.

It seems undeniable that the ego varies in importance, force and quality across different societies throughout history. And it is hard to distinguish the features of the masculine ego described here from what might be called the bourgeois ego. Da Vinci, both in his life and works, exemplifies the great Renaissance individual. And the beginning of the capitalist period certainly promotes the idea of the 'I' as self-sufficient and answerable only to itself. Having said this, one must add that the instinct for self-preservation is necessary, and so is some degree of self-love and the pleasure of narcissism.

Even the pleasures of trying to write an account of the masculine ego may be inextricable from the narcissism it describes. For what are the usual metaphors applied to a 'clear' analysis? Don't you try to keep out irrelevant things, put in what is needed, attack a subject vigorously by marshalling views in support, while all the time guarding against possible criticisms? This is another topic that will be opened up in a later section.

MAN AND NATURE

Come to where the flavour is

Marlboro Country

> *But his dominion that exceeds in this*
> *Stretcheth as far as doth the mind of man*

Christopher Marlowe

The masculine ego must try to master everything other than itself: physical reality both as nature on the outside and the body on the inside; other people in society; its own unconscious and femininity. This Marlboro advertisement shows how masculinity, in the dominant form, wishes to regard nature and landscape.

Although instantly recognizable, it is a complicated piece of work. The image is bound together by four horizontal lines linking: (1) mouth, cigarette and cigarette packet; (2) eye and the white typography ('Come to . . .'); (3) his hair and the horses; (4) the line of the horizon with its two mysteriously suggestive mounds or mountains. Two vertical lines run down through the man's head and body on the left, through the eye of the lead horse and the cigarettes sticking up from the packet on the right. In addition to the composition, two conventions help to unify the disparate parts of the photograph. One is the rule from strip cartoons that what appears in a bubble behind someone's head, joined to it by further bubbles, displays what they are thinking. Another comes from the editing of narrative films and dictates that two images juxtaposed are to be read in narrative sequence. Here the superimposition of the man on the landscape also tells us that the man is thinking about the landscape. The unity of the colour image helps to keep the government health warning outside the frame, literally on the margin.

Cigarette smoking is a pleasure for the mouth. Once again the distinction between bodily instinct and psychic drive is fundamental. Corresponding to areas of bodily pleasure – the oral and sucking, the anal and excreting, the genitals and sexual intercourse – there are forms of mental pleasure at the level of drive. In fact smoking is a good instance of the difference. The infant begins with direct satisfaction in sucking the breast and moves on to sucking the thumb instead. The child likes sweets and chewing gum; the adult tries to recapture infantile satisfaction through smoking and, with a sexual connotation, kissing. But smoking is mainly a narcissistic pleasure, especially in this advertisement. The man's face expresses composure and self-satisfaction, and if his features remind us of Robert Redford, this only serves to reinforce the idea.

His narcissism comes through not only in his smoking but in another deeply narcissistic pleasure, daydreaming. As his far-away look reveals, he is thinking of being a cowboy, the Lone Ranger, a Western hero. And this brings the image of the masculine ego in touch with nature. Here two very powerful myths come into play. One is the ancient myth that man is to culture what woman is to nature, that the sky and sun are male and the earth female. Another, much more recent, is the Romantic myth that man is most himself when he is spontaneously at one with nature. Several aspects of the image equate this man with nature and with that nineteenth-century child of nature, the cowboy (or cow-*boy*). His hair fades almost imperceptibly into the flowing tail and mane of the horses, just as the colour of his face runs into the red of the prairie. Cowboys roll and smoke cigarettes. And his jacket looks like a cowboy's leather, though of course in a much more up-market, Gucci mode.

Even though, as here, the masculine ego masquerades as being at one with nature, its true intention is to dominate nature. The world is presented as a natural dimension there only to be mastered. In the image, civilized man confronts untamed nature and takes up its challenge and invitation. Domination is implied by the smooth backs of the mustangs, asking to be broken and ridden. Once on the horse the lone male will have harnessed its previously unbridled natural power. Instead of running wild it will carry him in planned directions across the terrain. The landscape is all laid out, there to be traversed, because he can see – it is there in his mind's eye. Such mastery depends implicitly on his phallic power. His first finger points at the viewer, two cigarettes stand erect in his packet, the thrust of the cigarette in his hand, with its subtle touch of fire, links it and him to the horses. The three mustangs connote stud or stallion. And, so psychoanalysis claims, three is the phallic number because the male genitals consist of a penis and two testicles.

The mastery of the ego is narcissistic but cannot work without another object to master. The femininity of this landscape comes out perhaps in the warm, rich reds of desert and cliffs as they are lit by the setting sun. It comes out more obviously in the sexual associations of the canyon, the valley or cleft in the earth. And it is surely there on the horizon with its two, breast-shaped mountains. The feminine is there but it is contained and concealed, hidden in the margins. It was the same with the film *Red River*. Although the male bond was to the fore, in the end the conflict between fathers and sons was over the mother, giving energy to their quest. And like *Red River*, this advertisement is also beautifully photographed with the clarity and allure of a perfect, high-definition image.

Within the image, the man's contemplative self-possession dominates the activity of the horses and the passivity of the landscape because these are what he sees in his mind's eye. In the same way, a position of visual mastery is offered to the viewer of the image. In Da Vinci's castle a central point kept the whole layout under survey. In the titles for 'News at One', the camera position places the viewer so as to see the whole earth at once from somewhere outside, like the eye of God, which sees everything.

This position of visual mastery is a masculine one because it suits the masculine ego, as it does in the Marlboro ad. There are five separate parts of the image: the landscape, the horses, the man, the writing, the floating Marlboro packet. Partly through the composition, partly through the meaning, these are all brought together and unified for the viewer and his ego. An instant of time is frozen for ever – even the racing mustangs are. Except for the dust at the horses' hooves everything is seen in perfect focus and lighting – the pores of the man's chin, the hair on his little finger, the landscape through the perfect transparency of the desert air. In binding together the man in the foreground and the hills in the far distance, this photographic image operates according to the same principles of linear perspective as were developed by the painters who prepared the way for Da Vinci and Michelangelo. This is Renaissance space, bourgeois space, undiscovered by the ancient world. It is a dimension in which the masculine ego can move as fast as thought, mastering nature as far as the eye can see.

Probably some degree of identification with the mastery of the masculine ego is inevitable in our present culture. Within the photographic image we may identify with the domination the man exercises over the landscape by the very power of thought. In addition the image itself offers a position of visual mastery for which everything is brought together under an overriding gaze. Yet even in trying to set the operation of the masculine ego at a critical distance this present account does not escape its effect. The man masters the landscape. The viewer of the image masters him, the landscape and the image itself. Now we, reading the analysis, master the whole lot.

THE MALE BODY

This ordinary photograph, one that appeared in many newspapers at the time, displays the male body in the main form in which it is now celebrated, as an object of sporting interest. What happened in one hundredth of a second at the start of a sprint, when the athletes sprang from their blocks, is fixed for inspection. The five bodies are almost superimposed at an impossible angle, when the upward force of the start matches gravity at 45 degrees. What happens only as part of a cycle of relaxation and contraction is frozen into immobility – every line of every muscle from the jaw and neck, forearm and buttock down to the calf is drawn as tightly as a bowstring. Consequently the whole body is held together like a clenched fist. It is the moment of maximum effort privileged by almost every image of sport in popular culture, a privilege that is now coming to be granted to women, so long as they conform to the masculine ideal. We like to think of our bodies as being natural, but these five men, far from being outside culture, are deeply organized within it. They may seem animal but their bodies are carefully controlled to run straight down the white lanes towards the tape. In this image the masculine body is seen as existing for itself and against others.

The masculine ego must master everything. If the physical world on the outside can be overcome as nature, on the inside it may be dominated as the body, and an idea of the body. Real living bodies come in all kinds of shapes and sizes, and in ages from a day to a century. The physical differences between male and female bodies are relatively slight. Only one gene in eighteen is different, the rest are shared. From this welter of possibilities popular culture selects a certain stereotype to stand for the masculine body, from Michelangelo's *David* to Allan Wells, the Scottish athlete getting such a good start nearest to the camera in the photograph. The body is represented by the perfect young man, an idea that radiates out in at least five distinct directions.

For the masculine ego the body can be used to draw a defensive line between inside and outside. So long as there is very little fat, tensed muscle and tight sinew can give a hard, clear outline to the body. Flesh and bone can pass itself off as a kind of armour. The skin surface can take part in the masculine fascination with armour from ancient breastplate and greaves down to the modern American footballer, whose body subtly merges into strapping, pads and plastic plating. A hard body will ensure that there are no leakages across the edges between inner and outer worlds. Nature, it seems, has betrayed the perimeter of the male body. It has opened up there a number of gaps and orifices, though mercifully fewer than for the female body. What holes remain must be firmly shut, for as Norman Mailer makes clear in his war book, *The Naked and the Dead*, the first worry for men in combat is 'keeping a tight arsehole'. Tensed, the whole frontier can be kept on red alert.

Ask a child from ancient Greece to draw a person and the chances are they would draw the human body as a linked assembly of parts – calves, thighs, trunk, chest, hands, forearms, upper arm, and so on. Today in Western culture a child would almost certainly draw an oval with four lines coming out of it for arms and legs and with a circle on top for the head. So in our conception the head dominates the rest of the body as mind over matter. If, in the logic of Da Vinci's castle, the body is the ramparts, reason is the commander. For us this presupposes a deep split between the mind and the body, one the masculine idea of the body is particularly adapted to. It is to be the instrument of conscious will and intention. As Carl Lewis said after winning four gold medals in the 1984 Olympics, 'My body did everything I asked it.' He might have been talking about a horse or a car.

A number of aspects of post-Renaissance culture have contributed to this sense of the masculine body. One is a knowledge of anatomy (some of Da Vinci's medical studies are inaccurate, including the cutaway drawing of sexual intercourse). Divided into knowable parts the body can be reassembled as though it were a rational order – like Newton's solar system – or a machine. Discipline of the body spread from military drill in the seventeenth century to forms of prison punishment to training for manual labour, that is, work. Now that more and more people in the West are occupied in mental labour, an essentially masculine disciplining of the body has started to invade leisure – in athletics, gymnastics, jogging, aerobics, break-dancing. In every cultural image of these the same idea is present. Masochism, the pleasure of being hurt, perfectly combines with the narcissism of the masculine ego. If I can hurt my body freely, by an act of my own will, then my mind is proved to be master of my body.

The most important meanings that can attach to the idea of the masculine body are unity and permanence. As discussed earlier, the self finds its identity in a bodily image. Very clear in outline and firm in definition, the masculine image of the body appears to give a stronger sense of identity. From David to Tarzan and on to Superman, Captain Marvel, He Man, Action Man and Conan the Barbarian, the young male body is used to present not just the self as it is but as he would like to be, not just the ego but the ego ideal. – Super ego

As mentioned before, the infant loves its mother as itself. It identifies with its objects and cannot really distinguish its own identity as separate from them. That comes later as the ego develops. It does so because it begins to lose its first love and become aware of that loss, because a gap opens up between what it wants and what it gets, revealing that the world has its own real existence out there. Held up by its mother to a mirror the year-old baby may catch in its reflection an image of the identity it wants. But two identities develop, the 'I' and the ideal 'I'. As it loses the mother, the child imagines an idea of its former self that was perfectly loved, one different from its ordinary self. This former self gradually turns into a better self and this better self or ideal ego ends up watching you and telling you what you ought to do, being the voice of conscience, morality and the law. Images of the perfect young male body return to the masculine gaze a flattering reflection of how he would like to see himself.

So the pleasure of the usual representation of the masculine body is narcissistic. But these images of the hard, trained, disciplined body under rational control are not just there to be identified with – they are there to be looked at. They are styled for a masculine look in a particular kind of way. Allan Wells and the other athletes aren't striving only to please themselves, their own egos, but to please their better selves, their ideal egos. They are watching themselves in the same way as they're being watched. The masculine body is to be observed because it is under the eye of the father and wins his approval.

This brings up the question of how it is not to be observed. It is not to be looked at with the eye of desire. This is precisely the look the masculine body positively denies as though it were saying, 'Whatever else, *not* that.' The hardness and tension of the body strives to present it as wholly masculine, to exclude all curves and hollows and be only straight lines and flat planes. It would really like to be a cubist painting. Or whatever. But above all not desirable to other men because it is so definitely not soft and feminine; hairy if need be, but not smooth; bone and muscle, not flesh and blood. The masculine body seeks to be Rambo, not Rimbaud.

In the photograph the athletes are competing against each other. The most obvious aspect of these images of the body – Michelangelo's *David* was thinking of the death of Goliath – is that they express aggression towards others. The hard outline co-operates with this in several ways. It provides the notion of controlled aggression and discipline, the body under a watchful eye, an eye which is the eye of the father and of law. So aggression is legitimated. Then again the hard body disavows its vulnerability, as though every tendon and perfected movement were saying, 'It can't happen to me.' Partly the defined outline contributes here since it stresses the body as surface and conceals the weakness of the inside, or rather the insides. It makes us think of that Hollywood favourite, the flesh wound, and not think about damage to the bowel, the lung or the gullet.

Finally, one other thing completes the idea of invincibility. Not only is the masculine body invariably portrayed erect (the *David*'s bent left knee is unusual) but it seems to be able to inflate itself. When the body moves from relaxation to tension, 'the muscles grow in size, as they do for example when the ordinary little man turns into the incredible hulk or when Arnold Schwarzenegger plays Conan the Barbarian. Defying gravity in the high jump or the pole vault, puffing itself up like a bullfrog in the weightlifting, the masculine body can impersonate the phallus.

Defence of the realm

THERE is nothing unique about President Galtieri of Argentina. Our world is only too well stocked with land-grabbing dictators. They come in all political persuasions, in all degrees of mental instability, in all sizes.

They range from tin-pot tyrants with out-of-date second world war armour to oil-rich m a d m e n like Colonel Gaddafi and, at the top end of the scale, to the Soviet Union, super power predator of the planet.

As we value our freedom and the freedom of those who, like the Falkland Islanders, legitimately rely on us for protection, we must look to our defences against the whole motley and evil-minded crew.

The crisis in the South Atlantic will make Mrs Thatcher and her Ministers re-think the balance of Britain's defence priorities.

This is typical of the writing in the British press at the time of the war in the South Atlantic – the opening paragraph, six sentences, from an editorial in the *Daily Mail* of 7 April 1982. Nothing suggests that the nationalism in it is particularly masculine, especially since the very embodiment of nationalism is a woman, Mrs Thatcher. Even so, this kind of nationalism is masculine in the way it marks such a hard line between inside and outside, treating the body and the ego as fixed, self-sufficient. As presented here nationalism fits perfectly with the masculine ego and the masculine body, so that each overlaps and confirms the other.

Obviously, 'they' are bad and 'we' are good; they are 'evil-minded' and we are well-intentioned; they are 'madmen', character-ized by 'mental instability' while we are rational and 'look to our defences' while we 're-think' a balance of priorities. Reason, perfect vision and the rule of law ('legitimately') all go together. But it is not just that 'we' and 'they' are contrasted – it is rather that a really firm line is drawn between the two, a defended barrier, like the battlements around the self or the hard edges of the male body. 'We' are familiar, 'they' are foreign; 'we' are *inside*, 'they' are *outside*. In this version of nationalism, friend and foe, at home and abroad, are superimposed on an idea of the masculine ego and its other, everything outside that threatens it.

The metaphors carry a loaded meaning in the extract. There are four in particular: (1) 'well stocked'; (2) 'tin-pot'; (3) 'motley'; (4) 'crew'. President Galtieri is not 'unique' but one of many. 'Our world' – the one 'we' really own in the end – is a kind of shop or supermarket 'well stocked' with dictators. Like brightly coloured commodities they come 'in all sizes' that 'range from' one end of the scale to the top. A first feature, then, of this other side is that it is varied, shifting in size, as though its body kept changing shape. Secondly, it is 'tin-pot', a piece of tinplate masquerading as silver, and so it is false, an appearance not true to reality.

Other metaphors confirm this, in 'motley and evil-minded crew'.

For 'motley' is the word for the costume of a fool or jester, a suit of variegated patches. A third feature of the other side seems to be that it is an assembly of pieces attached together, not something coherent all the way through. And mention of a 'crew' takes this idea a bit further, for a crew – on a ship, for example – is an assembly of individuals who together are subordinate to the reason and command of a captain. And this in turn picks up 'mental instability' and 'madmen', and is developed by association with the irrationality of animals (like some lion or leopard, the Soviet Union is said to be a 'predator').

So, the other side is: (1) unstable, constantly varying in shape and outline; (2) a false appearance; (3) an organization made up from different bits and pieces; (4) irrational and animal. All this is on the outside and 'we' must defend ourselves against it constantly so that, in contrast, we, the patriotic male, can be: (1) single and undivided in body and ego; (2) true and real; (3) unified and solid, the same all the way through; (4) rational, subject to reason and law. As the opening sentence says, 'we' are 'unique', 'we' are one, 'they' are many.

'We/they' and the metaphors call on the reader to identify with a patriotism that is implicitly masculine. Now, ironically, the leader we are asked to identify with is in fact a woman. However, honorary masculinity is conferred upon her – she is 'the best man in the House of Commons', as they say at Tory tea parties. The phrase 'Mrs Thatcher and her Ministers' describes her as though she were God the Father with his ministers of grace, the angels. The nation is one and masculine and, according to this *Daily Mail* editorial, if I am masculine I am at one with the nation. Defence of the realm means defence of the masculine ego. Mastering the outside world through nature and the inner world through the body, it can hope to master others through the idea of nation.

Narcissism, Sex, and Masculinity

For psychoanalysis the two main forms of drive are self-love and sexual love for another. Part I of *The Masculine Myth*, 'Basic Masculinity', was mainly concerned with sexual drive; Part II, 'The Masculine Ego', was mainly about narcissism. In practice, however, they can't really be separated, and in the remaining sections we will find them overlapping and occurring together. And other varieties of drive will be discussed as they become relevant, particularly the oral, in relation to drinking, and the anal, which will be looked at in terms of male swearing.

PART III

MASCULINITY IN ACTION

MEN AT WAR

The Deer Hunter, directed by Michael Cimino (1979)

In a steel town at Clairton, Pennsylvania, Mike (Robert de Niro), Nick (Christopher Walken), Stanley, Stephen and Axel are friends. Mike, Nick and Steve are due to fight in Vietnam. Before they do, Steve gets married. At the wedding Nick gets engaged to Linda (Meryl Streep), and later gets Mike to promise to bring him back to Clairton if anything happens to him in the war. The next morning the friends go hunting in the mountains and Mike, as he hopes, kills a deer with a single shot.

In Vietnam Mike, Nick and Steve are captured by the Vietcong and forced to play Russian roulette with a revolver loaded with a single shot. Though he's very afraid, Mike compels Nick to play as part of a ruse through which they make their escape, taking Steve with them. Nick is rescued by helicopter, Steve falls and Mike goes back to retrieve him. All survive, though Steve loses his legs. Mike returns to Clairton where he begins to have an affair with Linda. Nick, however, stays in Saigon, compulsively playing Russian roulette.

Axel, Mike and Stan once again go hunting. This time, though, Mike has a deer in his sights but refuses to shoot it. He does threaten Stanley with his own revolver. Later he persuades Stephen to return from hospital to his wife in Clairton. He also finds out from him that Nick is still alive and, during the fall of Saigon, returns there to try to find him. Nick doesn't recognize him and once again Mike is forced to play Russian roulette with him. This time Nick kills himself after 'one shot'. At his funeral the friends gather sadly and sing, 'God bless America'.

Hailed as the film which helped America to face the war in
Vietnam and finally bury it, named as 'Best Picture' in the Academy
Awards for 1979, *The Deer Hunter* is not a typical war film in the
Second World War tradition. This staple Hollywood genre, from
The Sands of Iwo Jima to *The Guns of Navarone*, concentrated
mainly on war itself. Because Vietnam was a dirty war and deeply
unpopular, a variation of the genre is needed to make it acceptable.
So the war in South-East Asia is contained as part of a much
longer film about the community for which it was fought. This
more than anything explains the title and the four incidents that
link Vietnam with home: the killing of the deer with 'one shot', the
Russian roulette in captivity, the deer Mike doesn't shoot, the 'one
shot' that kills Nick. By interrelating the steel town and the war,
the film is able to turn a disturbing political scenario and history
into a tragic story of personal experience. At one point Linda says
to Mike, 'Did you really think life would turn out like this?' The
suffering of the war is transformed into the sad gain and loss of
growing up. And some kids don't make it.

Mike and Nick are buddies, a couple, and the rest, says Mike,
'are arseholes'. Mike is the masculine side. He has a beard,
invariably a hat, short dark hair, a long face and crisp, angular
gestures. He also, in de Niro's playing, has a habit of narrowing
his left eye to concentrate his attention. He accepts reality for what
it is and tries to control it, kill the deer with one shot. 'This', he
says, tapping his gun, 'is this.' Nick is more feminine, with smooth
skin, a soft round face, lidded eyes, long fair wavy hair. He talks
about 'the trees' and 'the mountains'. Faced with the necessity of
threatening his own life, he cannot accept this reality and remains
infantile, endlessly repeating the game with the revolver until Mike
brings him back to himself, he loses his childlike immunity, and
dies. Mike accepts the threat from the enemy, smiles as he pulls
the trigger at his own head, achieves self-identity, wins the girl and

rescues his buddies. At the end he is dressed as the Green Beret they meet in the bar at the beginning. Nick cannot face the threat of castration; Mike does and goes on to take the place of the father. The pain of war makes him an adult and a hero.

Defeat, Combat, Victory, Comradeship

As a masculine form in the dominant culture, war, whether in novels, films, or elsewhere, is structured round four crucial moments: defeat, combat, victory, and comradeship. Four traditional photographic images correspond to these. One is the horror of war, whether it is represented by the nightmare landscape of the Somme, the ruins of Hiroshima, or, as in *The Deer Hunter* at one point, by the squeaking of innumerable wheelchairs. The second image is combat – fighter aircraft and contrails in the Battle of Britain, marines on the beach at Okinawa. Thirdly there is the moment of victory, when the symbolic sons win an accolade from the father, riding in tanks through cheering Paris, having medals pinned on at the Kremlin. And, associated with all the others, there is the moment of comradeship, the picture of the soldier weeping for the fallen, comforting his wounded buddy. For psychoanalysis these moments or images are to be explained in terms of the fear of castration, the triumph of the masculine ego, fathers and sons, and the sublimated intimacies of the male bond.

Victory is absent from *The Deer Hunter*. It appears only in a muted and soured form when de Niro appears home in Clairton wearing his full dress uniform – and goes to a motel on his own, shunning the reception. The actual war sequences of the movie last less than half an hour. But they brilliantly capture and reproduce the other three elements.

A peaceful village nestles in the rich, green landscape. Helicopters suddenly appear and bomb it. Women and children hide in a hole in the ground. A member of the Vietcong appears, finds their hiding place and drops a grenade into it. For the civilians death comes from both sides. A mother with a baby crawls from the wreckage but the Vietcong shoots her. Pigs run off with the dead child. Mike, who has been watching the scene, fires his flamethrower at the soldier, engulfing him. More helicopters arrive, the Vietcong attack with mortars. The pigs fight over the dead baby.

It is a picture of 'the horror, the horror'. Partly it is an image of the body in pieces, literally 'blown away' as the contemporary soldiers' phrase said. But, since death is unknowable, the dread of death is a development of the fear of castration. And castration is the main fear behind the sequence which comes next.

Captured, the prisoners are forced to play Russian roulette, to point a revolver with one bullet in the chamber at the head and pull the trigger. A threat to the head and the phallic gun stress the idea of castration. The tiny, unsmiling Vietnamese commander for whose pleasure the game is played represents the figure of the bad father, that is, the father who enforces the threat of castration and offers no possible identification as the good father. The blood of the dead drips on the prisoners as they wait their turn to play, caged beneath the hut. Those who refuse are put in another cage in the river with rats, where they will drown slowly.

Nick says, 'I'm not ready for this.' Mike in contrast embraces a fate which is inevitable. He asks for three bullets in the gun, the phallic number, shoots his captors while Nick grabs another weapon, and they escape. Horror of castration under the image of death gives way suddenly to violent activity in combat. A threat is still present for they are under attack but are now able to defend themselves. They find a log, float downstream, keeping quiet while they pass an overhanging rock from which they hear the voices of Vietcong. The log snags on a rope bridge and they are able to scramble on to it – at which point they hear gunfire and a helicopter. One is helped aboard while the others cling to the landing skids.

Combat exercises a profound attraction to the masculine imagination, whether in fictional or documentary form. Michael Herr, for example, in *Dispatches*, the memoirs of a war correspondent in Vietnam, recalls how the fear of death while waiting gave way to the excitement of mortal combat when the fear was forgotten, a feeling, he says, like that of 'undressing a girl for the first time'. What common sense accepts as 'thrill' and 'excitement' needs to be understood and explained. Whatever real war may be like, its fictional version is made up of three components.

One is that in the dominant version of masculinity castration is never simply an accomplished fact. Because in patriarchal society masculinity is marked as possession of the phallus and its pervasive symbolic power, castration can never be more than a threat or a possibility. As masculine hero in the roulette game Mike has understood this and tells Nick that if he doesn't risk his head in the game he will still 'stay down here and die'. Believing in his heart that death is only a threat Mike takes the revolver and pulls the trigger. Here and in the combat which follows a second component must also be at work, that is, the mechanism of disavowal. The Vietcong, the enemy, represent a threat from outside, a fact which can be defended against by disavowal, pretending it doesn't exist or is not as bad as it seems. The castle of the masculine ego is much more deeply committed to defence through disavowal. From it issues a sense of invulnerability – 'It can't happen to me'. Even when facing almost certain death, Mike continues to believe that he can scheme a way out.

A third factor is the masculine ego's desire for mastery. Partly this is achieved through knowledge, knowing that three empty chambers leaves three full ones, enough to kill their captors (it is in fact a scheme as wildly unrealistic as anything Dennis the Menace might come up with). Partly it is achieved through mastery of the body since he kills the Vietcong with the same skill as earlier he had killed the deer. Bodily aptitude enables Mike to find the log, pull Steve on to it when he nearly drowns, climb on to the rope bridge, clamber up to the helicopter. And throughout the combat sequences the narcissistic pleasures of the ego issue in aggressive violence. Energy bound to make up the 'I' is released against everything that appears to attack it. The unity of the body is affirmed when the body of the other is destroyed, as though its motto in killing and mutilating were, 'I am everything so you are nothing – earth, a piece of shit, a dead body, a body I master by making dead.' This masculine narcissism is also mentioned in *Dispatches*. Michael Herr wonders whether the dead bodies they come across, some quite decomposed, are worse in the hot weather or in the wet weather. Then he concludes that the only dead body he couldn't bring himself to look at was the one he'd never see.

Legitimating the Male Bond

Mike's desire is for himself but also for others. In the cage he acts as good father to the others, calming Steve's hysteria, steeling Nick for their ordeal. During the escape he saves Steve from drowning, tries to help him up to the chopper and, when he falls, jumps after him. He nurses his appallingly broken legs ('I think I hit some rocks') and then gently hoists him on to his back and carries him until they reach a friendly column. For the rest of the film, despite his relationship with Linda, his thoughts remain with Nick. At great risk to himself he returns to Saigon as it is falling, as the 'shitstorm' hits it, and searches out Nick. When he finds him, Nick doesn't recognize him despite Mike's cry of 'Nicky, I love you, you're my friend.' So once again Mike risks his own life trying to relive the roulette and bring Nick back to sanity. At times Mike's sublimated homosexual desire seems to be less than fully sublimated.

The four elements of the war genre – defeat, combat, victory, comradeship – are not just a series but a structure. Defeat and combat, castration and narcissistic disavowal, are clearly organized in relation to each other, but so is comradeship. In the dominant versions of men at war, men are permitted to behave towards each other in ways that would not be allowed elsewhere, caressing and holding each other, comforting and weeping together, admitting their love. The pain of war is the price paid for the way it expresses the male bond. War's suffering is a kind of punishment for the release of homosexual desire and male femininity that only war allows. In this special form the male bond is fully legitimated. In the traditional Second World War film it is celebrated with the father's approval. With films about wars like Vietnam that is hardly possible. (There is always with such films a kind of 'victory' experienced by the viewer who identifies with the hero, who survives, as he usually does. This is a separate topic and will be considered later in terms of masculine style.)

A Matter of Life and Death

In writing about war it has been particularly hard to separate myth and experience, the fictions and fantasies about war from war as it is lived. One reason is that in practice women have been kept away from combat. For centuries Western culture, mainly on the paternalistic grounds that they are 'the weaker sex', has not allowed women to fight in the front line. This was not the case, however, in the Russian Army during the Second World War. And of course the spread of total war has meant women have been fully involved as civilians – in support operations, in espionage and resistance movements. In Britain after 1939 women were trained to fly Spitfires but only so that they could ferry them around the country. The aircraft were fully operational but because they were flown by women the planes were not allowed to carry ammunition. This information was not passed on to the Luftwaffe and from time to time a wandering Messerschmitt would come across a fighter plane flown by a woman. A number were shot down.

The subject of war also raises another issue. Without necessarily taking it for truth, I have been following the logic of psychoanalysis as a way to define masculinity. War brings this logic into a new area, one I mention only with some hesitation. Before 1920 psychoanalysis described human behaviour as motivated by two main forms of drive, narcissism and sexual desire. But after the First World War, a war in which over 60 million people were slaughtered, including members of his own family, Freud published *Beyond the Pleasure Principle*, a book in which he revised this view. Its argument is complex, speculative and extraordinary. It notes that some kinds of traumatic experience, particularly cases of shell-shock, could not be explained in terms of pleasure – either the pleasure of self-love or sexual pleasure. These two would not account for the way victims of war trauma suffered recurrent nightmares showing a destructive compulsion to repeat. On the same grounds that the drives of self-love and desire correspond to biological instincts towards self-preservation and reproduction, Freud was led to suppose that in addition to Eros there was also Thanatos. If there are instincts impelling us to live, there must also be a biological instinct compelling us to die, otherwise we would live for ever. Without actually naming it, he envisages a death gene that determines ageing and the end of life. To this instinct on the biological plane something must correspond on the mental plane, and that is the death drive.

It shows itself as a drive to master (*Bemächtigungstrieb*) – as when children pull wings off flies – and a compulsion to repeat (is this why old people lapse further and further into childhood memories?). Life emerges from a totally peaceful state of non-being, and it is the death drive that compels us in the end to repeat this, to return to the state of non-being. Along the way the death drive gets woven into other forms of drive, into sexual desire, the drive to master, masochism and sadism, and of course, feelings of aggression towards others, of which war is the most complete social expression.

The hypothesis of a death drive is undoubtedly the most controversial idea in psychoanalysis. Implausible as it may have sounded even in the material and moral devastation of Europe in 1920, it seems to have found appalling confirmation in the 1930s and 1940s, the Soviet Gulag and Nazi death-camps. And it returns as a terrifying possibility in the age of Cruise and Trident, SS 20s and 'collateral damage'. For the first time in human history our species possesses the capacity to destroy itself completely.

That is the historical possibility. In the meantime, though women in the West live on average five years longer than men, we all die. Every individual must submit to the death drive – if there is such a thing.

PLAY THE GAME

North Dallas Forty, directed by Ted Kotcheff (1979)

Phil Elliott (Nick Nolte) is a wide-receiver struggling to hold his place in the North Dallas football team. Having 'started' for six years, he now begins on the bench, partly because of a bad knee, partly because the coaches and management regard his attitude to the game as sceptical and immature. At a party he meets Charlotte Calder and with her begins to grow away from the game. After years of injury he has become reliant on pills and shots to get himself fit enough to play, and at one point he and his buddy, the quarter-back Maxwell, raid the team's medical supplies. They discuss their injuries and Max says he is getting to like the pain: 'When I dislocated my elbow it made me feel like I was doing something important.' Elliott cannot sleep at night for pain in his knee, shoulders, back and neck.

Delma, a young black player, is preferred to Elliott for the Chicago game. He injures a hamstring but refuses painkillers for it – 'all those pills and shots does terrible things to your body'. Elliott takes a shot and this persuades Delma to do the same, so he starts the game. The team psych themselves up in the locker room. Delma's leg gives out and Max persuades the coach to bring Elliott in. He scores a touchdown in the last seconds to tie the game. However, they fumble the snap on the pass back for the kick, so losing by one point. In the locker room afterwards the tackle, O. W. Shaddock, denounces the coach for turning the game into a job when it should be a sport played for enjoyment.

The owner, Conrad Hunter, calls Elliott to his office and terminates his contract, supported by Coach Strothers, who criticizes Elliott's 'childish attitude'. Elliott decides it is time to 'put away childish things' and leaves the game to join Charlotte Calder and raise horses on his farm.

Football is not a matter of life and death.
It's much more serious than that

Bill Shankly, manager of
Liverpool Football Club

Sport has helped to fill the gap opened up by the increasing split between work and leisure since 1850. Muscular team games, developed largely by the Victorian public schools in Britain with the combined aim of preventing masturbation and training young men to defend the Empire, have permeated every corner of the advanced world and beyond. Football and the English language can be seen as England's only lasting contribution to world civilization. Football or soccer began in the public schools and then was taken, with missionary zeal, to the industrial working class. It developed as a spectator sport when Saturday became a half-day, leaving the afternoon free. The Football Association was founded in 1863, its knock-out cup played for first in 1872.

Sport, especially since 1945, has become commercialized into an important earner in international capitalism. The World Cup in football and the Olympics, together with cricket, golf, tennis and a growing number of minor sports, are big business. Television has enabled them to become a spectacle in an unprecedented fashion, and a quarter of the world's population watch the Olympic Games. Sport is submitted to visual mastery so that an implicitly masculine eye is able to follow in slow-motion detail exactly how the pole-vaulter's wrist hit the bar as he fell. As it is represented in the dominant culture sport is deeply masculine, an arena to which women are admitted if they submit to its rules. Although sport is a staple diet of television, films about it like *North Dallas Forty* are surprisingly rare.

Before the Chicago game, while the North Dallas team kneel, the Monsignor asks for a 'blessing on these praying boys as they venture out to battle' until he is interrupted by Coach Johnson telling them to 'take off your fucking helmets'. Like war, sport as an expression of masculinity is organized around the four moments of defeat, combat, victory and comradeship. But unlike war, in which the rules state that the aim is to kill and maim, in sport the rules forbid injury. This doesn't stop Jo Bob Priddy and O. W.

Shaddock, the two enormous tackles of North Dallas, deliberately breaking the leg of an opponent who has continued to sack their quarterback. But it does change the structure for sport so that it becomes organized round the idea of the perfectly disciplined male body. Losing is not imagined in terms of castration but as the weakness of a masculine ego which failed to dominate its body. Victory, especially in team sports, enables the sons to win the approval of the symbolic father. At the same time the unified perfection of the male body becomes an emblem for nationhood. Despite his colour and rumours about his sexuality, the body of Carl Lewis, after it had won four gold medals in the Los Angeles Olympics of 1984, came to symbolize the United States itself.

North Dallas Forty

The basic meaning of this male-bond movie is set out in the first two sequences. It begins with Elliott waking the morning after the game and rediscovering, through a haze of pills and marijuana, the pain he feels in each part of his body and remembering, in flashback, how he was hit the night before. To an unusual degree this film stresses the bodily pain of sport. So it brings out very well how pain is the price for the male bond. The second sequence cuts to a lavish party held for the team. At this, except for Elliott who meets Charlotte Calder, women are treated merely as adjuncts to masculinity and what matters is the warmth of relation between the men. As Elliott leaves, Maxwell, the quarterback, glances at the makings of an orgy, saying 'it's the same old pile' and he's going to get in there.

The suffering brought to the body by this particularly brutal and dangerous sport is shown vividly in the preparations for the Chicago game. The players appear like walking wounded, who have to be taped, bandaged, strapped, given needle shots and pills and dressed in armour before they stop limping, their necks stop cricking, and they are psyched up ready for their opponents. Trying to persuade Delma to play with a torn hamstring, Coach Johnson tells him he doesn't know 'the difference between pain and injury'. It's a fine distinction. When Elliott is fired the chief coach tells him he's not put enough into the game. 'Not enough into the game?', he explodes, 'Christ, there's pieces of me scattered from here to Pittsburg on these football fields.'

The pain legitimates a male narcissism otherwise denied expression. The body is hurt but it is also a constant centre of attention from coaches, trainers, assistants, medics, owners, other players and women. In a sustained sequence Charlotte wakes at night and watches Elliott while he wanders half-naked round the room trying to work the agony out of his broken joints. Focusing itself on the male body, and indeed on the idea of the body in pieces, the masculine ego is fully exercised in the excitements of conflict: threat and mastery, retreat and advance, attack and successful defence. All the players love the game. Talking to Charlotte at the farm Elliott, the man with 'the best pair of hands in the league', describes what it is like to take the thrown ball despite the men trying to stop him. It's 'the feeling at the moment of the catch, the high' that he plays for.

Pain also legitimates an intensity of the male bond not easily available except in war. After the game and defeat the men comfort one another. One sits weeping silently, others murmur in pairs. Elliott crouches over Delma's stretcher, talking gently to him about his body. When O. W. Shaddock, the huge, bearded tackle, turns on Coach Johnson saying he treats the game as a job when it should be a sport with 'some team spirit', Johnson replies, 'You don't have to love each other to play.' The team clearly feels he is wrong.

On occasions the desire sublimated in the male bond threatens to spill over into a desublimated form. During the party at the beginning one player tries to take another's girl, they fight, but end up kissing with the quarterback commenting, 'boy meets boy'. The line between sublimation and desublimation is all the time defended, by, for example, the way the term 'arse' is used throughout, or by jokes. Maxwell the quarterback, Elliott's buddy, a country boy, says that nothing that happened at a party was really 'gross' – 'Gross is when you go to kiss your granpappy goodnight, he sticks his tongue down your throat.' Otherwise male homosexual desire is sublimated, as when Elliott comes on to the field and tells the quarterback, 'You throw it, partner, I'll catch it', or when

Maxwell looks admiringly at Elliott in the bath and tells him, 'You're the only guy I know got an uglier body than mine.'

In *North Dallas Forty* the father/son relation is worked out in terms of owners and players, capital and labour. The owners, Conrad Hunter Enterprises, would make more money by investing their capital elsewhere than in a football team, but that, as one says, wouldn't get them on the cover of *Time* magazine. The owners try to systematize the game through the chief coach, quantifying it in computer statistics, controlling plays from the bench, treating it as a job. The players want to play the game, extemporise plays and control the action on the field. When O. W. Shaddock denounces Coach Johnson he proclaims that he wants 'some team spirit', an idea which would have gladdened the heart of a Victorian public school headmaster. Told it is just a job, O. W. picks up the coach and throws him out, shouting that he and the owners are all 'chicken-shit cock-suckers'.

The narrative of the film closes when Phil Elliott comes to see his playing of games and the male bond that accompanies them as boyish and immature. Challenging the father, he wins his way to a mature relationship with Charlotte Calder. In fact the last image of the film can be read as his acceptance of castration. Max the quarterback throws a long ball to him in the street and he opens his hands to let it fall. In this dominant version, masculinity is presented through the aggressive achievements of the masculine ego, the male bond, and the relation to the father.

THE MAGIC KEG OF BEER

Television Advertisement for Greenall Whitley Beer (1985)

A scene from the old West. In a dry square with Mexican-style white buildings three men bound loosely with ropes round their arms and bodies are being led, presumably to a hanging, by a crowd of men who are shouting and shooting their guns. One of the three prisoners falls to his knees and all noise fades as he sings, 'I wish I was in Greenall Whitley land.' The shot dissolves to show a glass of beer being lowered on to a bar, and, as he sings of the girl he left behind, the camera shows a woman sitting sadly with another woman in a corner. However, as he sings about the other things he left behind – the warmth, the friends, the games 'we used to play' – one of the three friends shown, after chatting and smiling with his mates, goes over to the woman on her own, leans over her and obviously invites her to join him. As the song reaches the idea of 'games' the new couple are seen playing a pub game, the friend with his arm round the girlfriend.

At this point the shot returns to the present, as the singer continues, 'But most of all, Greenall Whitley, most of all, I'm missing you', leading to a crescendo in which the others (now five) join in as a chorus with 'Some day I'm going back to the taste I know so well'. The shot in the present begins as a close-up of the singer's face, now upside down, and slowly tracks back to reveal that the men, still bound, still with their hats on, are in fact hanging by their feet from ropes attached to the arch of one of the white buildings. Noise and shooting resume and in the sky in the background white Western-style lettering says 'I WISH I WAS IN GREENALL WHITLEY LAND'.

*A glass should never be full and
never be empty*

Irish saying

Oral pleasure in the form of cigarette smoking and the drinking of
alcohol has been marketed for many years, not least by means of
advertising like that in the Greenall Whitley advertisement. Along
with other drugs, alcohol has been used for thousands of years of
human history as a way of escaping unpleasant thoughts, especially
fear of death. In modern society drinking may have a historical
significance in that it is increasingly used to block the increasingly
nagging voice of conscience. This, the superego, can be defined as
that part of the personality which is soluble in alcohol. But in
addition to these conditions, drinking has a traditional meaning
attached to it as a particularly masculine activity and way of
celebrating the male bond.

This is how boozing is frequently represented in the dominant
images of men getting together. After arriving at Abilene in *Red
River* the cowboys head straight for the saloon and whiskey. And
The Deer Hunter shows almost continuous consumption of beer
during the men's hunting trip, as well as a significant example in
the representation of male behaviour, the drunken confession
between Mike and Nick. Alcohol makes permissible a personal
intimacy otherwise frowned on. As an image of masculinity,
drinking enables sharing even sometimes of the same cup. But in
the dominant tradition such celebration of male communion takes
place on rather difficult grounds. Quite simply, for masculinity the
idea of drinking and oral pleasure always brings up the idea of the
breast; and so the idea of the mother; and so the threat of incest
with which the image of the mother is always overshadowed (unlike
the little girl, the little boy moves directly from the mother to the
bride). In selling men the idea of oral satisfaction an advertisement
for beer must take them on a journey back, a regression, that can
negotiate a way past the mother and incest to the image of the
breast. One way to do this is to show the familiar figure of the
barmaid with swelling bosom behind the glasses of beer but with
the lower half of her body and its attendant risks carefully out of

sight beneath the bar. This Greenall Whitley ad takes another path and manages it very well. A great deal happens in forty seconds, aided by the fact that the little narrative fits into a set of other such ads we already know about. Some pretty threatening material is handled, especially in the idea of death by hanging, and so it has to be disarmed by being made into a joke both at the start and the finish. There is a harsh masculine irony when the condemned man, having presumably enjoyed the transgression for which he is being punished, falls to his knees and wishes he was safely away somewhere else. And there is another joke to conclude when the hung men aren't really dead but continue singing vigorously upside down and have hats that still don't fall off. Against this veiled threat of death and of castration the words and images set up the idea of another place immune to danger, Greenall Whitley land.

The ad shows two worlds. The present is not real but a fantasy from the Western, with dust, noise and conflict. The past is real in that the pub shown has ordinary, everyday life in it. And it is wet, represented by a pint of beer with a creamy head, while the present is dry. Nostalgia forms the link between the two worlds, present and past. And the little narrative offers the fulfilment of two wishes. One is to retreat from adult sexuality and the endless conflicts of fathers and sons, castrate or be castrated. Another is the positive wish to be safely back in a green, wet, conflict-free land. Nature, this faraway country, is, as always in the dominant myth, feminine. Here, it is maternal.

We get from one world to the other by means of the singer and the song. Though he is the tallest of the three prisoners, the singer, when he falls to his knees, is seen to have a square, rather boyish face with a curl on his forehead. And he sings solo in a high, clear, resonant voice, like a choirboy. The song itself is a ballad, its style reproducing the well-known theme of nostalgia from the take me back/my heart belongs/I remember genre. Here we are invited to return to beer with a milky-white froth on top, to the breast and the mother.

However, the journey back is fraught. On the way the bride is discovered, a nice girl, the kind you take home to mother, sitting with a very maternal sadness in her face ('Perhaps she's missing me as I'm missing her', he sings). But the anxiety this bride/

mother figure raises is quickly deflected on to the friend who interposes between the boy-faced singer and the woman, just as the father interposes between the little boy and the mother. At this point the whole scenario is swept aside. The theme of the song has moved ever backwards from 'the girl I left behind' to 'my friends' to the (childish) 'games we used to play'. Now it goes a stage further, beyond all these, rising to a crescendo with 'most of all, Greenall Whitley, most of all'. And the camera image cuts back to the present where the singer and his buddies, hanging upside down, dependent and immobile as babies, are happily singing their hearts out together. Of course the longing they express ('I wish I were . . .') is impossible. But the ad tries to make it possible. Veering away from conflict and adult sexuality it sidesteps bride and mother on its way to the paradisiacal breast. There, free from castration, the father, sibling rivalry, incest, the men are imagined to share communal bliss.

Action and Style

These three sections – on war, sport and drinking – have looked at the way some central forms of masculine activity are represented in the dominant culture. One could continue for some time in this vein, looking at the whole range of actions men are supposed to engage in. However, it is equally important to consider the style and language of such action, for this runs across many different kinds of behaviour. The next three sections look at three main varieties of masculine style in speech and writing.

Masculine Style (1):
Clarity

REVEALED:
THE GUN Pc

THE policeman whose gun killed a five-year-old boy was named yesterday as Pc Brian Chester.

And it was revealed that his past heroism had earned him a bravery award.

Last night the 34-year-old father-of-three was suspended on full pay following the weeking shooting of John Shorthouse.

The boy was shot in the chest as he lay asleep during a raid on his parents' home.

Yesterday John's mother, Mrs. Jacqui Shorthouse, vowed: "I will never forgive the man who killed my boy."

As she walked in a park with her two other sons, Danny, three, and Denis, two, she added: "I can't accept that it was a complete accident."

Pc Chester is staying at a secret address with his children and wife, who is expecting their fourth child.

His commanding officer, West Midlands Chief Constable Geoffrey Dear said: "The shooting has had a devastating effect on him."

Mr. Dear gave Pc Chester a glowing character reference, saying: "He is the very opposite of the gun-slinging macho image.

"He is everything I hope for in a policeman."

He added: "Not only did he win a bravery award, but he demonstrated his courage all the time.

"He volunteers to go on the sort of jobs when no policeman knows if the man on the other side of the door is armed with a gun."

The Daily Express, 29 August 1985

By law, even in the smallest seaside town, an Italian has the choice of the following daily papers: *Il Popolo* (Christian Democrat); *Unità* (Communist); *Il Manifesto* (Communist left-splinter); *Avanti* (Socialist); *La Reppublica* (Republican); *Il Secolo d'Italia* (neo-fascist); *La Lotta Continua* (Trotskyist). This is in addition to five or six 'independents' such as *Il Tempo*. In Britain, because of a different tradition, the freedom of the press means a choice between: *The Guardian* (liberal); *The Daily Mirror* (Labour); *The Morning Star* (Communist); *The Financial Times* (realistic Tory); *The Times* (high Tory); *The Telegraph* (militarist Tory); *The Daily Mail* (servile Tory); *The Daily Express* (extreme Tory); and *The Sun* (rabid Tory). Despite these political differences, and despite the contrast between the high cultural press and the popular press, almost all of these papers are written in one mainstream style.

The style of the extract from a report in the *Daily Express* of 29 August 1985 doesn't seem much of a style at all. It looks as though the story of Jacqui Shorthouse and Brian Chester is reported quite objectively, just as it happened. In fact this mode of writing, the clear or transparent style, did not exist in the Middle Ages, and in England was mainly developed during the revolutionary period of the Civil War by writers determined to argue clearly about religious and political issues. After that it became the dominant style, cropping up everywhere, not just in documentary reporting but also, by the nineteenth century, in novels. What characterizes the style is that it tries to be styleless, a clear window on to reality that presents the truth nakedly and objectively as it is, without any subjective feeling or attitude getting in the way. Arguably this is a *masculine* style.

Deborah Cameron, in an excellent book on *Feminism and Linguistic Theory* (1985), points out that language lets men and women say whatever they want and that there is no way one gender could control this. But within language there are different forms of *style* or discourse, and these can be contrasted as masculine and feminine. Mary Wibberley may have suggested one way to do this.

She has written a book, *To Writers with Love* (1985), which gives advice about how to write a romantic novel, with examples. One consists of the same sentence written in two different styles, and this is very useful because the meaning is more or less the same but the style is very different. Although she doesn't name it as a masculine style, she advises against plain and simple statement of fact. Instead of 'She didn't want to listen to him any more; she felt tired and weak – and tearful' the romantic novelist should write, 'She put her hands to her ears, tears of tiredness and weakness filling her eyes and spilling down her cheeks, and her soft golden hair tumbled about her face as she shook her head helplessly.' This calls attention to itself as a piece of style and clearly takes up an attitude to what it describes. The plain statement of fact pretends that it doesn't have a style and doesn't have an attitude to what it is saying.

This effect can be seen at work in the story about PC Chester. It appears to be simply a record, a statement of a number of facts. Though it treats these as if they were simply *there*, the story constructs its interpretation of what is really the truth and in a hidden way takes up a firm attitude towards it. It does this by giving two versions and then inviting us to discard one and retain the other as the truth.

In this respect the passage is rather like a court of law in which the prosecution and defence each gives their version but the judge and jury decide the truth. Here a man and a mother have different stories about what happened when the boy was killed. In one there was an accident, and the boy was killed not so much by a person as by a gun ('whose gun killed a five-year-old boy'); the man holding the gun is a hero with a bravery award, and also a family man whose wife 'is expecting their fourth child'. In an opposed version the mother says what happened wasn't 'a complete accident' and she can 'never forgive the man'. At this point a father figure emerges, Chief Constable Geoffrey Dear, whose words firmly decide between the two stories and in favour of the man, who is sensitive – the shooting has had a 'devastating effect on him' – not 'gun-slinging' but everything one hopes for 'in a policeman', having even won a bravery award.

Although the report in the part I've not quoted goes on to repeat more of what the mother has to say it weakens it by the way it is phrased – 'she believed', 'she claimed'. In contrast Chief Constable Dear 'said' the shooting had had a devastating effect, gave a reference and 'added' something else. The headline confirms his version, for it says 'Revealed: The Gun Pc' and there is also a photograph of the man smiling confidently at the camera with his hands folded behind himself over the caption 'Constable Brian Chester: A heroism award'. The report encourages the reader to dismiss the woman's version as partial and inadequate, and treat the other accordingly as the revelation of the truth behind or underneath it ('Revealed: The Gun Pc'). The effect is augmented by the contrast of two stereotypes, the hysterical mother and the brave hero. And we are encouraged to accept the truth behind the appearance because it is one often repeated in the British press, that despite everything the British police are wonderful.

There is no question of conscious manipulation about this effect of passing from a partial to a final truth. It is just part of normal, everyday journalism. But it does depend on treating the truth as simply *there* to be seen through a style which pretends to be completely transparent.

Truth as a Fetish

A style of apparently plain statement of truth without obvious personal bias is a masculine style because it goes along with the masculine ego and its desire for mastery. Truth in this style is presented as something to be fully known, seen in complete detail. Once again the idea of vision is central to the masculine ego. This masculine style is supposedly as 'clear' as water, as 'transparent' as glass. The point can be understood another way, in terms of disavowal and fetishism. It is a rather strange story, but one that will be needed again for later sections.

Almost always male, fetishists are people who find sexual pleasure in fetishistic objects such as elaborate corsets with lots of suspenders, furry knickers, black rubber. Freud treated a young man who could only be sexually aroused by a woman with a 'shine on the nose' (*Glanz auf der Nase*). This was his fetish, and Freud analysed it first by arguing that it really meant a look or *glance* at the nose. This look at the nose was a substitute set up in place of the mother's phallus that the little boy once believed in but did not want to give up. It was as though the boy discovered castration when he saw the mother did not have the phallus. But his look travels on up her body and makes looking at the nose a fetish, a substitute object for what he imagines she's got missing. Fetishism works through disavowal. The fetishist knows about the mother's castration but disavows it by pretending she isn't castrated, that the mother has the phallus in spite of everything. (The inevitable question is: *why does the fetishist, typically male, assume in the first place that the mother has the phallus?* It is a question that goes to the heart of patriarchy and will be taken up in a later section.)

Such disavowal of something in the outside world forms part of the defence system of the masculine ego, but defence working in terms of signs and meanings. All language, including the language of the *Daily Express* and its front page, has two separate aspects, sounds and meanings (what linguistics calls signifiers and signifieds). Because we have got so used to reading silently to ourselves we tend to forget that you can only get at the meaning of a word via its sound or a printed representation of its sound. And the transparent masculine style likes to encourage a reader to ignore the sounds from which we derive meaning. Just as the fetishist disavows castration, so the masculine style disavows the sounds of the words it depends on by treating itself as invisible, not really a style at all. In this way the clear style makes a fetish of meaning, presenting it as fixed, free-standing, closed round on itself. Truth is presented as objective and impersonal, something revealed once and for all and so there to be mastered and known. The truth, the whole truth and nothing but the truth, as they say.

Mastery and Fictional Truth

Our culture tends to make too much of truth. In the Western tradition, certainly since the Renaissance and to some extent stretching back to the Greeks, truth is treated as absolute, a be-all and end-all. This entails the disadvantage that we are likely to forget about the style and language in which truth is presented and the effect these have on a reader.

The styleless style of the *Daily Express* story treats truth as

simply there and so treats the reader as one who masters this truth.
The reader is implicitly masculine and has a number of positions
to identify with. In terms of his masculinity he may identify with
the man, the Pc, but in terms of his femininity he may feel
sympathy with the figure of the mother. Overriding these, no
doubt, is identification with the all-knowing father, the Chief
Constable, and probably, if this is not too subtle, with the *position*
of complete knowledge offered by the whole presentation, the
style, the narrative, and the characters in it. Now I'm fairly sure
the facts as reported by the newspaper are true, though with the
popular press one can't be certain. But one can ask how much
difference it would make if this story of crime and detection were
not fact but fiction?

If this were a story in a crime novel, it would be fictional.
Nevertheless, much of the effect produced by the invisible style
and mastery of what is narrated would still be generated. As
fictional truths detective novels are written in exactly this way to try
to give the masculine ego the pleasure of mastery, certainty, seeing
it all clearly laid out in the end. In fact classic country house
stories on the Agatha Christie model are told twice, once as they
happen to baffle all but the most perceptive reader, and then a
second time at the end when the detective *retells* the story so that
we can all follow it. Such forms of narrative give narcissistic
pleasure to the masculine ego.

They give this pleasure in another way as well, through the kind
of identification they allow to the reader. Any narrative, whether
fact or fiction, can provide this, though it is easier to understand in
the case of fiction. For psychoanalysis the pleasure of art comes
about because the human animal by nature seeks pleasure and
avoids what is unpleasurable. Unfortunately, the quest for pleasure
has to come to terms with reality. Children cope with this in one
way by playing games of 'let's pretend'. However, in our society
adults are not supposed to do this, though in other societies, such
as that of the Trobriand Islanders, or for us in the Middle Ages,
adult games of pretending were allowed. So instead of playing,
adults have daydreams that conform to the principle of pleasure by
acting out a wish. Not surprisingly these wishes are invariably
selfish or erotic or both, and almost everyone would be ashamed to

repeat them in public or even to a close friend. Art has a unique capacity to get round this difficulty. It provides the pleasure of wish-fulfilment, as do daydreams, but has a special power to disguise what it is doing. Instead of finding its fantasies boring or embarrassingly personal, we accept and share the chance art offers us to imagine the fulfilment of our wishes.

Probably art and fiction do a lot more than this. But the account points up one particularly masculine effect in many narratives – the presentation of a hero. If the story is realistic, if, that is, the fact that it *is* just a film or novel is carefully concealed, then the viewer or reader is invited to identify strongly with the hero. In films such as *Red River*, *The Deer Hunter* and *Dallas North Forty* the hero is central and the main point of identification. Such heroes not only do apparently exciting things and triumph over all kinds of threats, they also survive right the way through the narrative (if they don't it is a special genre called tragedy). So, for example, in the traditional Hollywood war film we know who's going to survive (heroes) and who won't (losers). From very early on in *The Deer Hunter* we guess that Mike is a hero and Nick is a loser, and are encouraged to place our bets accordingly. If we identify with Mike, then the working out of the narrative fulfils a strongly narcissistic wish, the wish that 'Nothing can happen to me'. Once again the masculine ego has things its own way.

But this can't happen unless a fiction puts forward its narrative as truth. It must hide the fact that it is made up if a viewer is to identify with the hero. Hiding that fact – trying to hide it rather – means using the transparent style, whether in novels, films, or television programmes. And something of the same masculine pleasure is offered to the viewer or reader even when the narratives are about fact, not fiction, as in the *Daily Express* story.

Of course, someone might well point out that, according to this account and definition of the clear style, this present book is written in a masculine style. Once again it seems that the structures of mastery associated with the masculine ego cannot be avoided in our culture. And certainly this book does try to be as clear as it can. At the same time there are two factors at least which call its truth into question, leaving its meaning open to debate rather than trying to close it on to something absolute and fixed, out there.

One is that the writing does not try to conceal the ideas and concepts by which it gets to its meaning. The other is that from the outset the argument has followed a political purpose – to unmask masculinity – that is openly avowed. Because that aim is explicit it can easily be argued against.

MASCULINE STYLE (2): BANTER

'The Long Ride Back to Scratchwood', an episode of *Minder*, the Thames Television series (1984, repeated 14 March 1985).

In London, Arthur Daley (George Cole), a second-hand car salesman who engages in shady deals, and his bodyguard or 'minder', Terry McCann (Dennis Waterman), enter a scheme with a young man, Justin, to make money by selling football tickets in Scotland for the England/Scotland match at Wembley. An ageing player, Steve Benson, has acquired 2,000 tickets at face value (£8); Justin wants Arthur to stake the deal for £18,000 (not £16,000) in the expectation that they can be sold well above face value on the black market. Normally such deals are organized by Phil, the King of the Touts.

In a sub-plot, Terry is called to the office of the Income Tax, where he finds to his surprise that Arthur has been claiming expenses of £1,500 per year to pay Terry as his gardener. Terry confronts Arthur with this news.

Much against his better judgement Arthur agrees to deal with Justin and Steve Benson, and makes contact with a fierce Scotsman called Alasdair Fraser. Having collected the tickets from Wembley they all drive north, followed by Phil and his heavy sidekick. At a motorway caff Phil confronts Arthur; at the same time Alasdair phones Scotland and discovers the tickets are forgeries, for which Benson is responsible. Phil is placated, the forgeries are destroyed, the deal called off and Arthur will get back his £18,000. He will of course be out of pocket for the interest on it (3% for 48 hours, then 3¼% per day), as well as the expenses of the trip north.

> *What passes for wit in* Minder *would be laughed off the stage in Glasgow*
>
> Robbie Coltrane, Scottish comedian

Banter or repartee is not an exclusively masculine style. It is used between friends and between lovers. But it is used so much and so often as a form of male exchange, it is so widespread and powerful, both in life and its fictional representation, that it must be considered an example of masculine style. As such it can be analysed into three features, one governing its mode of operation, the other two its content. As humour or comedy, banter makes use of every kind of irony, sarcasm, pun, clichéd reply, and so is an example of the joke (this is discussed later in another section). The content of banter has a double function. Outwardly banter is aggressive, a form in which the masculine ego asserts itself. Inwardly, however, banter depends on a close, intimate and personal understanding of the person who is the butt of the attack. It is therefore a way of affirming the bond of love between men while appearing to deny it. The analysis is straightforward, but banter or repartee figures so largely in masculine style that it needs to be looked at in detail. There are two examples here, one of the father/son relation, another of the elder/younger brother.

The publicity still for *Minder* exhibits clearly enough the symbolic relation between these two men. Terry McCann, wearing casual clothes and an open-necked shirt, is smiling boyishly at the viewer. Arthur Daley, besuited and wearing a tie, smiles paternally, pats the young man on the back, and smokes his ever-present cigar. A cigar obviously enough is able to serve as a phallic symbol, but so is a tie, for it has the special attraction, as Freud points out, that each man can choose the shape and size he wants. Terry is the son who has not challenged the father and remains stuck in a relation of passive sublimated desire for him. Much of the banter turns round his dependence on Arthur.

A television series such as *Minder*, watched regularly by 13 million people, has a basic situation which runs across episodes, though each episode has one main story. Arthur goes back a long way but Terry, as the title reminds us, is a one-time boxer who has been to prison for an act of violence. He needs a job from Arthur who, though constantly under suspicion, has never actually been convicted. The series works with a lot of Cockney wit (a man is said to have 'more front than Selfridges', the Oxford Street store with a grotesquely Baroque façade), as well as London regional prejudice (in 'The Long Ride Back to Scratchwood' Arthur looks despairingly at an ordinary Midlands landscape and calls it a 'wilderness'). The ideology of *Minder* affirms a special kind of working-class conservatism. Its tenet is that the whole economic system is a hypocritical fiddle so it is up to individual members of the working class to look after themselves as best they can. Interrogated by the Inland Revenue, Terry admits that he pays no tax, collects no dole, pays no national insurance and has no social security number.

Besides the contrast between father and son, Arthur and Terry are opposed in other ways. Arthur represents mind and capital, Terry body and labour. Arthur is dishonest, self-deceived, vain, rhetorical – Terry honest, realistic, pithy. Yet Terry needs Arthur, both financially and emotionally, more than Arthur needs him.

For both, women are problematic. As befits the son, Terry has an idealistic and rather gallant attitude towards women but, despite the occasional brief encounter, has no lasting relationship. Arthur greets any general reference to women with an anxious, wrinkled expression, and refers to his wife as ''er indoors'. They are much more interested in each other than in the opposite sex, and the titles for the series perfectly sum up their love-hate relation. The titles show a series of stills with the two bickering and arguing. But on the soundtrack a jangling and raunchy title song says that 'I would be so good for you' and 'love you like you want me to'. The tension and intimacy of their relation expresses itself as banter and is partly resolved by this, as some examples from the episode suggest.

Talking about Terry's news that young Justin has a proposal for him, Arthur says, 'I don't like young people – I certainly don't want to meet one of them.' Consciously or not he is attacking Terry, who is of course young, and Terry replies, 'He's not "young people", he's a person, ain't he?', so putting in an implicit plea for himself and his desire to be recognized by the father. Arthur sneeringly asks, ''Ave you seen them?', as though all the younger generation are self-evidently awful. Terry looks out of the window of the car and says, 'There's one, there's another one – look at that one, that a girl', mocking Arthur's view that young people (such as himself) are members of an alien race. The aggression of Terry's banter is obvious but it also assumes an affectionate intimacy with Arthur, recognizing his (Arthur's) fears of getting old and, in part, his fear of Terry.

In cold print jokes that play very well on screen and in a situation look contrived and forced. But the same tensions operate inside other examples of banter, such as when Arthur is defending himself to Terry and Justin against the accusation that he sold someone a stolen Mercedes. Arthur says he didn't know it was stolen and the court believed him: 'Judge says I was a mere *prawn* in the game.' Terry punctures this protestation of innocence with 'Jury says you were a prune!' Within an aggressive cover this conceals the close knowledge that Terry has of Arthur's self-importance and effeminacy. But it also reveals Terry's fondness for Arthur's weakness and the fact that his aggression is only verbal, as it is in Arthur's lame reply, 'I still got off with a £300 fine.'

When Alasdair Frazer, a name, as is pointed out, that rhymes with 'razor', arrives from Scotland, Arthur tries to save money on a hotel by getting Terry to put him up. Terry refuses on the grounds that "E growls, and 'e mutters and then 'e attacks', adding that he had 'three fights' last time Alasdair was down. Later it turns out that Alasdair is staying at the Holiday Inn at Swiss Cottage. Arthur says to Terry, "E don't growl, do 'e?' and Terry replies, 'Not yet.' Outwardly Arthur is getting at Terry to prove he was wrong about Alasdair and outwardly Terry is saving face by pulling a reply out of the hat when not much is available. But inwardly much more is at stake. Arthur is apologizing to Terry for exploiting him but also seeking reassurance for his own cowardice and terror of physical violence. Terry's reply reminds Arthur of his dependence on Terry's boxing skills which, though not yet needed, may well be called on before Alasdair is safely back in his Scottish lair. Before that, however, there is a sub-plot and the matter of Terry being named as Arthur's gardener to be tidied up.

In a long string of jokes Terry conveys the accusation to Arthur, whose only concern is for himself and having made a false tax declaration.

TERRY: You bin sussed.
ARTHUR: You didn't grass on me did you?
TERRY: 'Course not. Anyhow, what do you know about grass, eh? 'Aven't even got a bleeding garden, have you?

The pun on 'grass' is straightforward enough, and so is Terry's aggression, though it is this piece of repartee which effectively disperses his anger in the rest of the exchange. But once again hidden depths in the relationship are brought into play – Arthur's timidity and fear of the law, his trust in Terry. And Terry is aware that Arthur doesn't know about grass because he has never done a day's labour in his life and that in any case the garden exists only in Arthur's gentrified imagination. In banter explicit aggression between two masculine egos covers the implicit male bond. Such apparent aggression would not be allowed to an outsider. It depends on a covert and affectionate awareness of 'how like you that is'. And much of the viewer's pleasure depends on appreciating this.

Banter between Brothers

If the repartee in *Minder* negotiates a relationship between father and son, that in *On the Ball* expresses the feelings between brothers. *On the Ball* is a half-hour football programme previewing the afternoon's games and the news of the week. It intersperses clips and announcements, but instead of having simply an anchor man it has developed a team of two, Ian St John and Jimmy Greaves. This is the only programme on television in which the technicians laugh. Greaves's mordant wit has won the programme three million viewers and driven the BBC's competitor to compete from another slot. Greaves and St John are buddies or symbolic brothers, and this is now becoming a favoured form for television news and commentary because it allows ideas to circulate in exchange between two men.

As a form of working-class culture football in Britain works very much through regionalism. It also draws heavily on nostalgia, and memories of a younger, fitter body and younger, fitter men. Both aspects are focused in the contrast between St John and Greaves, and the assumed knowledge about them the viewer must bring to the programme. St John is Scots, played for Liverpool, a northern team, and in his time was a mid-field grafter of considerable prowess. Greaves, a reformed alcoholic, is a Londoner who played for Tottenham Hotspur and was a forward with one-touch brilliance. Wearing a suit and a tie, St John represents the respectable working class and the elder brother. Greaves never wears a tie and represents a cheeky, younger, less respectable brother who has more fun. Three jokes from a single transmission (of 27 March 1985) are enough to suggest how banter works between these two.

Noting at the beginning of the programme that Greaves is wearing a pullover made up from a dazzling array of different coloured wools, St John remarks that people will be 'adjusting their sets'. Gently needling, this draws on the knowledge of Greaves as a flashy personality, both in his private life before reform and in his style of play. But it also allows Greaves to explain away the jumper by saying that it was presented to him 'by a Scottish goalkeeper who dropped it on the way in'. This is very close banter and its point is lost on those who don't know that Ian St John is Scottish and that Greaves has for some time been running the accusation that Scottish footballers only score goals because the keepers are so bad. The joke both gets at St John and acknowledges his identity from a position of personal intimacy.

Later, St John, who has a remarkable capacity for keeping a straight face, mentions the coming performance of Liverpool in the semi-final of the European Cup. He says he is glad they have not drawn Juventus but will meet the Greek team, Panathenaikos. Greaves jumps in with, 'You said that well, sir', drawing attention both to St John's new-found middle-class ability to pronounce foreign names and the bland way that he has slipped in mention of his old team's success.

Having watched a filmed interview with Mike Channon and Asa Hartford, two players who made their name in the 1970s, St John comments, 'Nice to see Mick and Asa still there', a line which gets at them by noting that they are still alive. Greaves adds, 'Very nice – two players of our generation, Saint.' This is a double joke, because firstly it makes St John and Greaves out to be players of the 'seventies, when they were in fact of an earlier generation, and secondly because it presents Greaves as a contemporary of St John when in fact he is in reality the older of the two. The line both affirms a bond between the two and asserts the ego.

Banter or repartee as a masculine style is effective because it operates a double bluff. Because it is comic and relies on the joke form it appears to be genial, permissive and open. It is not in fact genial because it actually works with the aggression of the masculine ego. And it is not open because it sets out to protect and reaffirm the male bond – sublimated homosexual desire.

MASCULINE STYLE (3):
OBSCENITY

Will Darnell in 'Christine', directed by John Carpenter (1983)

Arnold Cunningham, a bespectacled teenager, buys a dusty and neglected 1958 Plymouth 'Fury' called Christine. He cleans her up in a huge garage owned by Will Darnell. Later in the film Christine starts to show a will of her own, becomes enamoured of Arnie and kills people who threaten him.

Will Darnell is unshaven, balding and has a double chin; he chews gum and spits; he wears a loose collar and tie and a dirty green jerkin over a fat belly. When Arnie first brings the car into his garage he calls it a 'piece of shit' and a 'mechanical arsehole'. He also recalls that he knew someone who was killed in Christine, adding that 'the son of a bitch was so mean if you'd put boiling water down his throat he would have pissed ice-cubes.' He lets Arnie keep the car in his garage but warns him, 'you screw around with me one time, I throw you out on your arse.' Then he shambles off, scratching his bottom as he goes.

Later, watching Arnie cleaning Christine, Will comments to his father that Arnie has been doing 'all this shit' for three weeks and has even got 'fucking brand-new windshield wipers' for the car. The father says Arnie has got good hands, to which Will replies that he's got bad taste in cars, adding mournfully, 'You know, poppa, you can't polish a turd.' He tells Arnie off for taking spare parts from a junkyard at the back, saying, 'Don't think you got the gold key to the crapper', and reminding him that without his good will it would cost 'a whole shitpile full of dough to put this heap together'. He then softens, noting 'you ain't exactly got money falling out of your arsehole', and offers him work picking things up round the place, 'Shit like that'. Arnie says he'll think about it and Darnell concludes with, 'Don't think about it too long, I'll throw you out on your fucking arse.'

Later, when Christine goes on the rampage, Will Darnell goes after her with his shotgun. He climbs inside and is squeezed to death against the steering wheel when his seat unaccountably moves forward as Christine's radio blares a hit from the 'fifties, 'Boney Moronie'.

In a novel by Dostoevsky a group of drunken men roll down a street at night frequently using the same monosyllabic Russian word. With different intonations it means quite different things – angry exclamation, a reproach, intense feeling, admiration, surprise, envy. The word is of course the Russian equivalent of the English 'fuck'. The incident shows how hard it is to generalize about swearing and how much the meaning of prohibited words depends on their context.

This said, some points can still be made about swearing as a style. The first is that it is a masculine style, as Mailer implies. Though obviously women swear, probably they swear less than men and in a different way, and men are not supposed to swear in front of women. The actual forms swearing takes are cultural and historical, and seem to depend upon what is most highly valued in a society. Swearing in the Elizabethan period relied on the value attached to Christianity. All the strange invocations of parts of Christ's body – 'God's blood' and 'God's lights', and so on – assumed high reverence for the idea of Christ crucified. Although blasphemy persists in modern society, it has been largely supplanted with swearing by genital and anal functions. Such swearing is clearly transgressive, a deliberate effort to break the rules of politeness and good verbal behaviour.

As transgression swearing is aggressive, and so an exercise of the masculine ego. Aggression is particularly apparent in the repetition of 'fuck' as verb, adjective and noun, often several times in one sentence. In this way the word may recall its relationship to the German word, *ficken*, to strike. 'Fuck' generally presupposes that an active male does something to a passive female. Genital swear-words – cunt, prick, balls, twat – have taken on a fixed, abstract quality in modern culture. In contrast, at least on the evidence of Eric Partridge's marvellous book *Shakespeare's Bawdy*, the Elizabethans had at their disposal two hundred synonyms for the male genital organ and another two hundred for the female, as well as hundreds more for what happened when they came together. Modern sexual slang is mechanically repetitive. It tends to turn sexuality into a fixed object, yet not even a complete object but a part of a person, a defined and limited part of the body. If this masculine discourse does tend to treat sexuality and women as things, the effect can be explained and will be referred to in a later section on photographic images of women.

Like everything else, swearing has a historical character. In Britain it has a strong class meaning with obscene swearing having the connotation of being especially working-class, officially regarded as vulgar by the middle class and often as a natural expression of freedom by working people themselves. National cultures also have different patterns for swearing, even when they use the same language. In North America 'son of a bitch' is widely used where in Britain one would expect 'bastard'. In American English 'bugger' has little force. It can even be used to mean 'eavesdropper', as for example when someone in Coppola's film *The Conversation* refers to an expert in electronic surveillance by saying, 'He's the best bugger on the West Coast.' So the position of 'bugger' in transatlantic vocabulary is taken by 'arse' and written and pronounced 'ass'. It is used to mean something like 'self-love fixed anally', and gives rise to phrases like 'Move your ass', 'I'm going to have to kick ass' and so on.

As a masculine prerogative swearing seems to extend to masculinity the same freedom to explore and exploit language as does nature, as was suggested in an earlier section. While oaths derived from genital sexuality are hard to bring into clear focus, a more precise account can be given of words drawing on anal ideas, especially with help from Will Darnell in the example. This is the appropriate point at which to look at masculinity and the anal in general.

Masculinity and Anal Eroticism

Some parts of the body more than others are likely to cause pleasurable excitement. As well as the mouth and the genitals, obviously enough sources of physical pleasure, there are the surfaces lining the inside of the anus and the urethra. These, and the musculature around them, are stimulated by the passage of faeces and urine. If we keep in mind the distinction between instinct and drive, we can see that the possibility of psychic pleasure can correspond to the physical stimulus. For the developing infant the importance of the anal stage is encountered after the oral but before the discovery of the genital. Its pleasures are never fully set aside by the adult, whether male or female.

The idea that anality is attractive may appear quite absurd, a sick joke. But, prejudice aside, we ought to recall the behaviour of dogs, and for that matter of young babies, who clearly love squidging and squirting when they have their nappies changed. Freud suggested that in the early history of the human species sexuality had a powerful anal component as it does with dogs, but that this gradually became lost. And as an instance of the quirkiness of desire and the arbitrariness of disgust he gave the example of a man who would kiss his lover passionately on the mouth but couldn't bring himself to use her toothbrush. Jokes, rude postcards and swearing are all good examples of how much interest we all have in the anal. One reason for this is that sexual feeling can very easily attach to the anal so that it becomes erotic. Manifestly, people who practise buggery find the anus a source of sexual pleasure. And so to some degree do people who use an everyday phrase such as 'to go like buggery'. If the whole range of human activity is considered dispassionately it should not seem so exotic for Rimbaud to write a lyrical poem to 'The Arsehole'.

Anal eroticism affects men and women in three ways especially. Pleasure can attach to the idea both of the active expulsion of faeces or urine and to that of being passively penetrated. Secondly, since producing a turd is one of the first ways we learn to control ourselves and our bodies, different meanings can be symbolized by giving up or keeping faeces. Surrendered, they can mean a gift ('Do it for mummy') and so an expression of sexual desire; retained, they embody narcissistic pleasure, something we want to keep for ourselves. Either way, faeces represent a gift and money, as is evident in common phrases about 'having a pile' and 'rolling in it', or being 'filthy rich'. All of this may lend an unexpected interpretation to the well-known television advertisement in which a James Bond figure overcomes incredible difficulties (skiing down steep mountains, jumping off trains) in order to sneak into a woman's bedroom and secretly leave behind for her a box of (black) chocolates.

A third aspect of anal eroticism concerns tidiness and order. Dirt is matter in the wrong place. And so getting rid of dirt by putting it in the right place yields an anal pleasure, or rather, it sublimates anal eroticism by turning it to another end. Piling up money through the effort of putting things in order is doubly a form of anal eroticism and, as has often been remarked, has a close association with capitalist accumulation and enterprise.

So far the pleasures of the anal may apply to both men and women. Both run together the anal and the genital whenever they refer to 'the bottom', and young children persistently confuse the two, believing that babies are born through the anus. But it is the view of psychoanalysis that while men seek to separate the genital from the anal and maintain an opposition between them, women are much less concerned to draw a firm line. If this is the case, there may be several reasons for a male wish to reject and exclude the anal. The most obvious one of course would be that through the idea of penetration and being penetrated the anal focuses male homosexual desire. To a would-be perfect masculinity, anal eroticism must be rejected along with the femininity of which it might become a bearer. Less powerful feelings bring the anal within range of the masculine ego. Clearly, if there is a choice between giving something away in conjunction with sexual desire or keeping it, narcissistically, for yourself, the masculine ego will prefer the latter. And the same ego will welcome the sublimation of anal pleasure into the narcissistic form of keeping everything in its place. Cleanliness, order and discipline are the watchwords for defence.

But anal eroticism cannot be escaped, any more than Dennis can finally dump Walter. The pleasure of cleaning up depends upon being dirty in the first place, just as you can't enjoy tidying something unless it is a mess. By the same logic, anal swearing tries to exclude the anal but can only do this by recognizing it as well, by expressing it. The attempt to expel the anal means it always comes back, and with erotic meaning attached to it.

Will Darnell's Foul Mouth

Will Darnell, in a bravura performance by Robert Prosky, swears in a way which perfectly illustrates the ambivalence of this masculine feeling about the anal. His words show that he both wants to get rid of dirt and keep it as something to love. For him the car Christine is both a dirty object and a prize to cherish; money is both wealth and power, and filthy lucre. Arnold, the seventeen-year-old youth, is both a cause of pollution and, as it turns out, an object for Darnell's desire. Swearing acts out this double movement, which it is particularly adapted to do because language can both name something and deny it in the same breath.

Darnell keeps saying things in a way that suggests their opposite. Calling the worn-out car a 'piece of shit' seems an obvious enough rejection of it, but adding that it's a 'mechanical arsehole' suggests that it is bad because it is mechanical, and so doesn't provide the pleasures of a real, sensitive human anus. Similarly, the extraordinary and rich metaphor of the man who swallowed boiling water and 'pissed ice-cubes' also implies two things. There is admiration for the total bodily mastery and self-control of this mechanical man whose body was like a machine for dispensing ice (like those that line the corridors of American hotels). But there is also the idea that pissing lumps of ice rather than warm, liquid urine would be as unpleasurable as drinking boiling water.

Watching Arnie clean the car, Darnell seems to condemn him for doing 'all this shit', but the mention of getting brand-new windscreen wipers shows that really he also likes and respects all the 'shit' he has been doing. His astounding epigram, 'You can't polish a turd', tries to reject the anal but only by regretting that you can't keep your faeces for ever, as shiny and glossy as a brand-new car. Another negative, 'Don't think you got the gold key to the crapper', asserts how nice it would be if you *did* have this golden, phallic key. Arnie doesn't have *money* falling out of his arsehole but he does have, by implication, something Darnell finds much more attractive, excrement. Finally, his desire for Arnie comes to the surface when he offers him a job, doing things round the garage, 'Shit like that'. Rejected, Darnell repeats his threat to throw him out on his arse. He really wants Arnie to 'screw around' with almost as much as he doesn't.

Darnell's sexual desire is centred completely in anal eroticism. By swearing he keeps trying to separate the genital from the anal, and above all to expel from his uncontaminated masculinity his homosexual fixation on the anus. He hates what he loves and keeps trying to eject it, just as he threatens to throw out Arnie. Of course it constantly returns, just as, to consider the other end of the story, eating food constantly replenishes the supply of faeces. Perhaps this is why, in the narrative, Darnell, the fat man who is always chewing, gets squeezed to death by Christine to the sound of 'Bony Moronie'. The double movement he represents and expresses in his swearing must also be an effect for the spectator of the film. Will Darnell is a dirty, ugly, aggressive and unpleasant character, but he is also vividly memorable. Watching the movie we too like him and hate him.

PART IV

THE SAME SEX

MASCULINE OR HOMOSEXUAL

Servicemen sold military secrets

for sex and drugs, says QC

HOMOSEXUAL ORGIES 'SPAWN SPY RING'

SEVEN young servicemen, who took part in homosexual orgies, betrayed hundreds of military secrets " of the greatest sensitivity " while serving in Cyprus, it was alleged at the Old Bailey yesterday.

Their ringleader, GEOFFREY JONES, a senior aircraftman, used the other six's homosexuality to lever them into becoming spies, said Mr MICHAEL WRIGHT, Q C, prosecuting.

But, ironically, it was Jones who led to the spy ring's downfall by his infatuation—with a woman.

The Daily Telegraph, 11 June 1985

*When I lived in Bermondsey . . . we had a saying,
Bermondsey was a place where men were men, and women
counted as 'manholes'; and members of the 'Middlesex
Regiment' would not be tolerated*

Anonymous letter to Peter Tatchell,
Parliamentary candidate for Bermondsey
in 1982

The account of sexuality given by psychoanalysis assumes that
the human infant is polymorphously perverse, exploring without
inhibition any possible avenue and site for pleasure. It also recognizes that the adult does not give up all its early pleasures but
rather keeps his or her bisexual potential. Men's divided sexuality
has been seen in all the examples so far considered, and these
have only dealt with men as they relate to themselves and as they
relate to each other. Taking the way masculinity is represented in
popular culture, my argument tried to show that in the dominant
myth masculinity contains no particle of femininity but is simply
one and the same all through.

Again and again the traditional version of masculinity contradicts
itself. The great male symbol, the phallus, turns out to be more
interesting to men than to women. Psychoanalysis is able to show
that the supremely masculine relation of fathers and sons has a
strongly homosexual component. Male femininity could be seen at
work in what boys aspired to be – and not be – as well as in many
other traditional masculine forms of activity – war, sport, drinking,
banter, swearing – at least on the evidence of the examples and
images discussed. Such femininity has to be dealt with somehow, if
the myth is to sustain itself.

One way to cope with it is to try to throw it out. This is
particularly a task for the masculine self. The masculine ego has to
defend itself from 'the enemy within', and this mainly takes the
form of its own femininity. Similarly, the male body defines itself
as a closed surface, trying to exclude what contradicts its supposedly
seamless masculine unity. And the example of anal swearing
showed another type of the same contradictory process. A man
kept trying to speak of shit as something that was bad and should
be got rid of but kept finding it was something he liked because it
was erotic.

The dominant myth of masculinity demands that male homosexual desire, if it cannot be sublimated, must be expelled. And this governs the prevailing attitude towards male homosexuals. It accounts for homophobia, the fear of homosexuality, and for the way that gay individuals are made into scapegoats, getting the kind of abusive anonymous letter that Peter Tatchell received during his period as prospective candidate for Bermondsey and recorded in his book, *The Battle for Bermondsey*. Homophobia directed against males operates by trying to impose a series of binary opposites. The first term is meant to override and exclude the second. Most important is the opposition masculine/homosexual. But this becomes superimposed on other oppositions, especially natural/ unnatural, and with particular application to the body, healthy/ sick. Another key pairing, one that relates homosexuality to social group, is national/alien; another, using race, is white/black. Inside/ outside corresponds to all of these but has particular application to the body and the aim of separating genital from anal, and ensuring desire does not touch the anus.

Obviously the opposites come to pieces in your hands. The first term is meant to *exclude* the second. But it can't because it can only be defined *in relation to* the second, and in fact depends on this other term. Nevertheless, homophobia strives manfully to eliminate its opposite, the thing which causes it. It does this mainly through three operations which are understood by psychoanalysis as projection, hysteria and paranoia. These explain why the dominant myth attacks homosexuality with such excoriating ferocity.

The Three Mechanisms of Homophobia

Psychoanalysis has permeated Western culture this century far more than is usually noticed. One of the concepts from it that has gained most currency is that of projection. This rests on a distinction between subject and object, internal and external. Projection names the effect by which something that threatens an individual from within can be imagined as a threat from the outside. A young child who feels aggressive towards his parents may invent a giant who is going to stamp on them. The father of a teenage daughter may externalize his incestuous desire for her by supposing every teenage party is a sexual orgy. Projection can also work socially. In Nazi ideology the supposed humiliation of Germany after the First World War was turned into anti-Semitism, and a group such as the Jews imagined to be dirty and abject. So, clearly, a masculine fear of homosexuality will be turned outwards into homophobia.

Although hysteria has a familiar, everyday meaning, as a term in psychoanalysis it is technical and precise. It seeks to explain hysterical symptoms, that is, illness that now might be called psychosomatic. An example might be paralysis of the arm for which there was no physical or organic cause, as could be demonstrated if the patient were able to move the arm when hypnotized. It is not so much the arm as the idea of the arm that is paralysed. The explanation would suggest that the arm has become a site for two contradictory repressed wishes, as it would be if the patient on the one hand felt angry towards their father and wanted to strike him with the arm, and on the other felt love towards him and wanted to touch his genitals. So that neither shall happen, the arm must stay still.

At a deeper level the opposed wishes or fantasies of hysteria are understood as flowing from the masculine and feminine sides of the individual. Hence the idea of homosexuality is likely to excite hysteria by bringing into play both sides of an individual if these are felt to be opposed. And of course they are in the traditional opposition of masculine/homosexual. The tension of hysteria can be seen, for example, in the kind of extreme and contradictory writing in the letter to Peter Tatchell. If 'men were men' surely women would be women. But no, they are something much more strange, 'manholes', suggesting simultaneously the female genitals and holes in men or holes men fall down. Despite first appearances, the news report from *The Daily Telegraph* expresses directly contradictory feelings.

Homosexuality will always excite an extreme response from the dominant myth of masculinity. It will provoke hysteria. But it will also attract something more dangerous – paranoia. Fear of homosexuality is always likely to be projected as the fear that homosexuality is attacking you from all around in the outside world. But the connection is closer than that, for, in the psychoanalytic account, paranoia actually *derives* from homosexual desire.

The little boy moves – if he does – into predominantly heterosexual desire under the threat of symbolic castration. However, if he does not fully accept castration he can get stuck, as it were. The threat of castration can get repressed and so, along with it, can his femininity and sexual desire for a masculine object. To the extent that it becomes repressed rather than sublimated into the male bond, his homosexual feeling is likely to return. And defence against it can cause paranoia. The process can be described in terms of four stages or statements in which one feeling is transformed into another. The first is homosexual desire, (1) 'I love him'. But the attempt to ward this off turns it into its opposite, (2) 'I do not *love* him – I *hate* him'. The mechanism of projection changes it into another equivalent statement, (3) 'He hates me, which justifies me in hating him'. Generalized, this becomes, (4) 'I do not love him – I hate him, because he persecutes me'. These transformations try to explain what is noted as a main feature in paranoia. For it is the most loved person of their own sex that the paranoiac fancies as their chief persecutor.

Seemingly implausible, this analysis may seem less implausible in an example. George Orwell's novel *Nineteen Eighty-Four* is quite simply the most widely read novel published in English this century, and to date has sold over 11 million copies. It has also recently been made into a most successful film with Richard Burton. It is not hard to read it as a paranoiac fantasy, since its hero, Winston Smith, lives in a world which he thinks constantly attacks him from all sides. The central figure of this world is Big Brother, whose pictures seems to menace Smith from every poster and hoarding with the words 'Big Brother is watching you'. Smith is attracted towards his boss, a man called O'Brien, and thinks he can plot with him to revolt against Big Brother. But O'Brien turns out to be an agent of Big Brother, and spends the last third of the novel torturing Winston Smith. Curiously, however, Smith hardly resents this, and in fact at one point of particularly extreme pain realizes, 'He had never loved him so deeply as at this moment.' His worst persecutor is precisely the member of his own sex he most loves. And so also it proves with Big Brother. Throughout the novel Smith thinks he hates Big Brother. But at the end, in the very last sentence of the book, Smith realizes, 'He loved Big Brother.' The defence against homosexuality has gone. And so has his paranoia.

The novel illustrates exactly the structure of paranoia as theorized by psychoanalysis. And it suggests also how readily homophobia in the form of paranoia can lead to violence and aggression. The novel suggests something else. Because homophobia is the projection of what is felt as the enemy within in the guise of the enemy without, it always has a strong cultural meaning and content. Homophobia, particularly when it leads to paranoia, always gets bound up with ideas and fears about social groups, nations and classes. In the example to be looked at here, gay behaviour becomes part of the Cold War and appears as dangerous as the Soviet Union, Reagan's 'wicked empire'. There is no need to multiply examples. Towards overt homosexuality the male myth has one response and only one: homophobia.

A Headful of Tights

It would have been depressingly easy to find a more extreme example of homophobia than the *Daily Telegraph* news story at the beginning of this section. Reports about AIDS in the tabloid newspapers in early 1985 would have provided more lurid and obviously hysterical instances. This comes from a middle-class paper, and mixes its own journalistic summary with the legal discourse of the prosecuting counsel. It is written in the masculine style, aiming for complete clarity and knowledge. It is all factual, or at least as factual as anything a prosecuting counsel says at the Old Bailey (the jury later decided, in October 1985, that facts were not true, for all were then acquitted and a public inquiry set up to discover why charges had ever been brought in the first place). In the report there is a rational, conscious and factual level. But as was argued earlier in connection with the example of clear, masculine style, this kind of objective and rational account aims to set aside many irrational features that come into play. Underneath the masculine factuality, this is an occasion for fantasy. Fears about the loss of state secrets become interwoven with homophobia. At this level the real threat to national security is posed here by male homosexual desire. The enemy without is really the enemy within.

The appeal to fantasy is brought out in the headlines, particularly the word 'spawn' and the emphasis on 'homosexual orgies'. And the top headline is totally ambiguous, since selling 'secrets for sex' should mean both 'in *return* for sex' but also means '*about* sex'. That the reader is likely to read the story as fiction rather than for its facts comes out in another way. The QC says later on, 'It is a thoroughly unattractive story.' And officially the reader is supposed to think the same. But this unattractive story is in fact told twice, once here, and once on the front page. The total coverage runs to 106 column inches, which is why it cannot be cited in full. In fact the main point is summarized in the headlines and the three sentences quoted.

Besides the clear elements of paranoia – the nation under threat and so on – the writing is hysterical because it is so tensely contradictory. At the literal, factual level it corresponds to masculinity in the official version: this is a crime to be condemned. But all the time images and metaphors are used which subvert the official seriousness. A feminine level in the writing describes homosexual desire in a way which becomes comic and indulgent. The report finally condones what it means to condemn. When the usual oppositions are used, variations on masculine/homosexual, they tend to come undone.

Masculine/homosexual are opposed in terms of nature and the unnatural. Homosexual orgies 'spawn' a spy ring, a metaphor which treats humans as animals, frogs, and female animals at that, since it is the female frog which lays eggs in the form of spawn. Possibly the word 'spawn' in conjunction with the white rings in which frogs lay their eggs suggests 'sperm'. The opposition masculine/homosexual also corresponds to what should be known and what should not be known, to knowledge and secrecy. Homosexuality is the secret of masculinity that must not be made known. What the QC calls 'the very heart of a most sensitive military establishment' is not so much military technology as homosexuality. That is what has to be defended against, the secret that has been 'betrayed', or as the headline says, one of the 'secrets for sex' that the masculine myth must deny.

Masculine/homosexual is supposed to separate inside from outside, but the line has been broken. There has been 'a breach in security', 'a major leakage of classified information' so 'channelling' it to foreign agents. The solid demarcation of the male body has turned to water, its closure broken by cracks and fissures. Liquid keeps on oozing, or as the QC says of the passage of information, 'the flow was constant'. Without meaning to, this metaphor ties in with one of the factual elements of the story, which is that the homosexual orgies were known as 'splash' parties.

Masculine here is to homosexual as real life is to false performance or pretence. One metaphor asserts that doings of the group were 'orchestrated' by one of them, and this idea of performance carries over into otherwise factual references to a contact who was 'said to have been a theatrical agent' and the involvement in the story of a 'cabaret singer'. The 'spy ring' comes to sound more like a circus than a conspiracy. Clean is opposed to dirty, when it is reported that one of them 'fell foul' of the investigation. Dirt and the anal is still on a reader's mind when they reach the factual detail that information was passed in an envelope left 'behind a lavatory cistern'. Control is set against loss of control when one victim shows 'unbridled enthusiasm'. Masculinity is at home, homosexuality is abroad, for the main foreign agents were a Cypriot and an Arab.

Although the official and correct way to read the story would give weight to the first terms of each opposition – masculine, natural, knowable, inside, real, clean, controlled – the actual effect of the story is to reverse this weighting. A kind of comic reversal runs right the way through, from the male homosexual who became 'infatuated – with a woman' to 'an Arab named John' and to the mention of a 'splash' party at which the chief accused 'disguised his identity by wearing tights over his head'. One man was at a homosexual orgy because, so he says, 'I did not want the regiment to think I was queer so I went along.' In this kind of context even the wholly factual names of the accused become symbolic, for there is Lightowler, Payne, Glass and Tuffy. The QC is named, of course – Mr Wright.

As an example of homophobia the *Daily Telegraph* report means to repress homosexuality by putting to work the usual structure of binary oppositions. But the risk is always that the repressed returns. What is intended as a solemn judicial judgement cannot stop itself becoming carnival. The judge's wig turns into a pair of tights as this hysterical condemnation of male homosexuality gradually becomes an expression of desire.

Masculine Essence/Feminine Essence

So far, Parts I, II and III of this book have been concerned with masculine relationships. The argument has pursued the insight of psychoanalysis that male sexuality, like all human sexuality, is unevenly divided and has a bisexual potential. It has looked at the various ways the dominant version of masculinity treats masculinity as undivided, and so must find means to deny, exclude and contain male femininity and homosexual desire. Part V considers how relations between men and women are represented and symbolized. Here the same preconception of a single, seamless idea of masculinity is upheld, but in a different strategy. The aim is to put forward masculinity as a pure essence defined against what is wholly other than it, femininity as a pure essence. Men and women, male and female, masculine and feminine are to be compartmentalized, sorted into opposed categories and assigned to separate places.

Inevitably the strategy comes apart at the seams. It comes undone in two different respects – on the outside and on the inside. In the outside world the masculine myth tries to contain the feminine and the idea of woman by keeping it subordinated and in place. But it will never stay fixed where it is put. At the same time, inside the individual, the myth of perfect masculinity continues to be undermined. The other side of masculinity keeps coming back.

Patriarchy can be defined as a system in which women, not men, are exchanged in marriage. But who is doing the exchanging and what do they feel for each other? The dominant idea of masculinity is sustained in a symbolic system based on the phallus. But how can the system ensure that the phallus is never an object of desire for the masculine individual? In each section and each example – the use of photographic images of men and women, the romantic love relationship, male jealousy – the masculine myth faces different problems. But the consequences are the same.

PART V

MASCULINE/ FEMININE

Exchanging Women (1): Marriage

He for God only, she for God in him

John Milton on Adam and Eve (1667)

Tucked away in the Church of England prayer book for hundreds of years, this list of the people you can't marry seems pretty bizarre today. What granny would ever contemplate marrying her grand-daughter's husband unless this table said she couldn't? In fact some of these prohibitions have been lifted in recent years. Yet, sanctioned by organized religion and inscribed in the law of the land, this list represents a very British variation of the universal law of human culture which prohibits incest. It reads like the findings of anthropologists who have worked on the kinship systems of a primitive tribe and found out the particular code the incest taboo takes in that society.

In one respect the table of forbidden affinities does represent something universal, the law of human culture that the infant must grow up and take his or her place in adult society by giving up love for the mother. In another respect, however, the list is not universal but patriarchal. It pretends to equality between the sexes in the careful symmetry by which those a man and those a woman may not marry are lined up opposite each other. In fact it is no accident that the left-hand column comes first, 'A Man may not marry his: – Mother'. For there to be a taboo on incest either the men or the women from one family must marry into another, or, as in primitive societies, from one clan into another. Patriarchy decrees that it is the women who are objects of exchange in marriage and not the men. Thus the prohibition on incest is imposed in the name of the symbolic father.

A dictionary defines patriarchy as: 'social organization marked by the supremacy of the father in the clan or family, the legal dependence of wives and children, and the reckoning of descent and inheritance in the male line'. Patriarchy clearly has a social foundation in the way families, tribes and societies are organized. And it has always tried to incorporate into this the biological basis for gender, particularly by making women especially responsible for childbirth and nurturing. But it is the psychological and internal aspects of patriarchy which are the main concern here. The need to prevent incest means that sexual intercourse between close relatives must be forbidden. To do this through an exchange of *women* is a patriarchal solution. It leads on to a symbolic system which treats the father as supreme and tries to make masculinity universal by defining sexual difference in terms of a male symbol, as plus or minus the phallus. Women are clearly visible as the objects which are exchanged but much less visible, although equally important, is the male bond between the exchangers.

The Phallic System in History

There are many ways in which Freud's account of the unconscious is permeated by masculine assumptions. One of the most obvious is that it presents itself as universal rather than as what it is, an analysis of patriarchy. So it is with his assumption that the taboo on incest, some form of which exists in every human society, always follows the same pattern of the ancient Greek story of Oedipus, the king who killed his father and married his mother. In *Totem and Taboo* (1912–13) he tries to explain the origin of all human society in a single event. The first father kept all the women to himself and so, to gain brides, the sons had to kill him and eat him. Later Freud came to concede that this was a 'scientific myth', a kind of 'Just-So' story like the ones in Rudyard Kipling. For it *presupposes* just what it pretends to explain, which is why it should be the father who had all the power in the first place.

Anthropologists such as Bronislaw Malinowski have challenged the view that the incest taboo always takes the form Freud assumes, a desire for the mother prohibited by the father. In *Sex and Repression in Savage Society* (1937) Malinowski describes the culture of the Trobriand Islanders in Melanesia. In their family structure property is inherited by the male child from his uncle, his mother's brother. The boy's relations with his mother and father are close, friendly and relaxed. But there is a strong taboo on incest with members of the uncle's clan, and specifically the boy's sister. Because of such evidence the French anthropologist Claude Lévi-Strauss worked out a much more general notion of the nature of incest. Whatever particular objects are forbidden by the rules governing incest, its importance lies in the very fact that it does lead to rules and conventions. While incest might be perfectly possible in terms of biology (the supposedly disastrous genetic results are much exaggerated), it was made impossible by laws and institutions. Incest is forbidden because in this way nature and natural instinct are denied while human culture and social obligation are affirmed. It is significant that this repeats in another form Freud's distinction between biological instinct and symbolic drive.

Even if incest taboos do not universally correspond to the model Freud describes, they certainly do in Western culture. The son desires the mother and competes with the father for supremacy, as he does again and again in the stories of the ancient Greek gods. Uranus imprisoned his sons in a kind of pre-emptive strike. But his son Kronos, at his mother's instigation, rose up and castrated him. Kronos in turn ate all his children except for one, Zeus, who was saved by his mother. Zeus defeated Kronos and took his place as ruler of Olympus. There he lives on in a troubled relationship with his wife, Hera. Christian mythology provides a much more radical solution to the problem of competition between father and son for the love of the mother. God has no wife but creates everything, and Jesus, far from challenging the father, suffers the worst that can be done to him. Women are simply written out of the script.

Based on the idea that the only way to solve the universal problem of incest is through the exchange of women, patriarchy continues in different forms throughout the Western tradition. Although it clearly has an embodiment in a social organization and laws which decide the legal dependence of wives and the way property is inherited, it is much more than this. It is a symbolic system through which the laws are lived by individuals. So it defines masculinity by two related principles. The first is that gender is determined by possession or non-possession of the phallus. The second is that masculinity must find itself in the place of the father or not at all.

Mike's Smile, or the Phallic System Explained

When Mike in *The Deer Hunter* is forced to shoot at himself, he puts the loaded revolver to his head and smiles. He thinks he is invulnerable, partly because the masculine ego is able to disavow threats from the outside, including the threat of castration. But partly also his confidence comes from the idea that he possesses the phallus, an object of such cultural power it can never be finally destroyed. The phallus is able to take on this meaning in the dominant culture because it serves to represent sexuality itself and also the difference between the sexes. In a masculine culture the inevitable loss of the mother, which falls on both sexes, is symbolized as the loss or lack of the phallus. And sexual difference is defined in terms of having and not having the phallus so that women are always seen as somehow *more* castrated than men. Hence the imbalance Freud describes by saying masculinity encounters castration as a threat, a possibility, while femininity recognizes it as an accomplished fact.

Freud's account is weakened and lends itself to being completely misunderstood because it keeps using the language of biology. For example, it refers to the penis as though it were an organ of the body that was in question. In fact, the instinct/drive distinction should require a consistent use of the term phallus since what is at stake is a symbolic idea. It is, however, very clear that Freud is writing about a symbolic system when he refers in the account of fetishism to the mother's penis that the little boy believes in. One reason for preferring Jacques Lacan's discussion of masculinity is that it consistently uses the term phallus, so making it explicit that a symbolic system is at issue. He also does this to bring in Lévi-Strauss and his emphasis on human culture as going beyond nature. Lacan analyses the way a patriarchal culture puts the phallus at the centre. He describes phallocentrism as a purely abstract symbolic system, and, in doing so, how the inherited tradition defines masculinity in relation to femininity.

Just as in Freud, the little boy demands the mother for himself, is threatened with castration, and so transfers his desire to the bride. But Lacan understands castration much more radically as a symbolic event, in fact as an effect of language and the way the infant enters language to become a child who speaks. Re-casting castration in relation to language complicates the whole account.

Before castration the little boy does not have the phallus. Rather he *is* the phallus for the mother. She has the phallus in having him and so makes up for what she lacks (this is indeed the phallic system in its pure form). The boy in loving her seeks to be fully present for her and at first treats language as though words were completely full of meaning and he could speak himself perfectly to her. But he discovers gradually that she desires in him what she has not got, the phallus. And so, wanting to be what she desires, he comes to recognize his own castration or lack. The discovery is bound up with the discovery that words are not things but only *names* for things, empty of full meaning. The boy also comes to understand that the father is not the perfect father he imagines –

he begins to separate the real father from the symbolic role he only imperfectly performs. He discovers that the father is not a real presence but a name. So the boy gives up wanting to be the phallus and seeks to have the phallus. Castration, lack, the recognition that words are only words and paternity only a name, all these work together to encourage him to take up his own place in the system as father and possessor of the symbolic phallus.

Lacan's reworking of the castration complex in terms of the name of the father – the discovery that fatherhood is only a name – does find support in some prominent features of patriarchy. One is the use of patronymics in different societies, so that people are named after the father and the father's father and so on. Another is that naming children after the father solves the old problem about paternity. 'It's a wise son who knows his own father', as the saying goes. And so if nature cannot provide proof of who a baby's father is, then in the name of the father law can step in and decide paternity. The father's name is also crucial in the exchange of women since daughters take the name of the father and then, as brides, the name of the bridegroom's father. However, Lacan's explicit, purely schematic account of how masculinity is supposed to work in the phallocentric system points out very well where the system undoes itself, or contradicts itself.

Three Contradictions in the System

In the dominant conception of it, masculinity tries to disavow and deny what it depends on. Very obviously, in the exchange of women, masculinity depends upon women to be exchanged. A second difficulty emerges if we are asked to think of castration and the making of masculinity in terms of the name of the father. Plausible as this seems, it poses a problem that can be posited as a pretty simple question: if the father is a name, why this name when any name would do? Once again the argument leads back to a single essential question: why should everything seem to begin with a male symbol in the first place? And again this issue will be left over for the moment.

What is so useful about Lacan's account of 'the name of the father' is the way it points to a gap that opens up between the supposed reality and the name, and how masculinity has tried to fill it. The masculine myth keeps coming back to the idea that the father is absolutely *all there*, that sons are perfect copies of him, that they are masculine all the way through, and that fathers and only fathers are really responsible for making babies. In ancient Greece this myth appears in the story of Athene. Zeus was frightened that Metis, his first wife before Hera, would bear him a son who would overthrow him. So he swallowed Metis when she was pregnant. The child, Athene, was born out of Zeus's head. This is not the only male maternity in our culture, since Jesus in the Christian story is born from a father who dispenses with the normal decencies of sexual intercourse with a partner. Jesus is an even more perfect embodiment of the masculine myth since the father creates him purely as an idea, by an act of speech, renting a womb from an unwilling virgin.

In contemporary popular culture the myth of male procreation is hidden inside a film such as Hawks's *Red River*. As was pointed out, the John Wayne figure seems to acquire a son out of thin air. And he continues to offer himself as the complete father, origin of his own name and the brand of his ranch, rather than as simply a person who bears a name. For a long time the symbolic sons accept this, presumably because they want to believe in that kind of father. It is only with some pain that they give it up.

Thirdly, Lacan's analysis supposes a kind of essence of masculinity and femininity. Sexuality is determined around the idea of the phallus, and only in relation to it (him). Masculinity is that which has the phallus and desires the feminine. Femininity lacks the phallus and so desires to have it in so far as it is represented by the masculine. And this is a close analysis of the model the dominant version of masculinity tries to impose. He for God only, she for God in him.

We have been here before (see Part I). The idea that men are masculine and only masculine because they possess the symbol of male power, the phallus, only works if it can guarantee that the phallus is not an object of male homosexual desire. It is, as is demonstrated by something else in the system. If patriarchy consists of the exchange of women between the fathers and between fathers and sons it must assert the male bond. And this is motivated by the homosexual desire which is expressed in all forms of male relationship: between fathers and sons, between men at war and at play, and in various forms of masculine style. The exchange of women can only repress the feminine without by expressing the feminine within.

This account of masculinity and phallocentricism has all been fairly abstract, though the later discussion of examples from popular culture will put some flesh on these bones. It has been important to look at the system clearly, as though it were a piece of algebra. But the very next section turns well away from the abstract to the particular. It is also concerned with exchanging women and how masculinity treats femininity as an object. But its example is one very special form in popular culture, that of jokes.

EXCHANGING WOMEN (2): JOKES

The 'Chinaman' Joke from 'Chinatown', directed by Roman Polanski (1974)

(Jake comes into his office from the barber's, opens the door smiling, speaks to his two associates.)

JAKE: Duffy! Hey, Walsh! *(to secretary)* Sophie, go to the little girl's room for a minute please.

SOPHIE: But Mr Gittes . . .

JAKE: Sophie!

SOPHIE: Yes, Mr Gittes.

DUFFY: Jake . . .

JAKE: Listen to me, man, I want to tell you a story. So there's this guy . . . Walsh, you understand? . . . he's tired of screwing his wife.

DUFFY: Jake . . .

JAKE: So wait a second, Duffy, you're always in such a hurry. So his friend says to him, 'Hey! Why don't you do it like the Chinese do?' So he says, 'Well, how do the Chinese do it?' And the guy says, 'Well, the Chinese, first they screw a little bit, then they stop and they go and read a little Confucius; come back, screw a little bit more, then they stop again, go back and they screw a little bit more . . .

WALSH: Jake . . .

JAKE: Walsh, just listen to me for a second. *(Walsh looks behind Jake to the door at which appears Mrs Mulwray, grey suit, grey hat; she watches and listens to the story)* You'll love this. Now, then they go back and they screw a little bit more. And then they go out and they contemplate the moon or something like that, makes it more exciting. So now the guy goes home and he starts screwing his own wife, see. So he screws her for a little bit and then he stops and he goes out of the room and he reads *Life* magazine. Then he goes back in, he starts screwing again, he says, 'Excuse me for a minute, honey', and he goes out and he smokes a cigarette. Now his wife is getting sore as hell. He comes back in the room,

he starts screwing again, he gets up to start to leave again to go
look at the moon, she says, 'Hey! what's the matter with you?
You're screwing just like a Chinaman!'
(*Jake cackles with laughter*) Jesus! (*Jake begins to turn slowly and sees
Mrs Mulwray; he looks at Walsh, who shuts his eyes.*)
MRS MULWRAY: Mr Gittes.
JAKE: Yes.
MRS MULWRAY: Do you know me?
JAKE: Well, er, I think I would have remembered (*supportive
agreement from Walsh in the background*).
MRS MULWRAY: Have we ever met?
JAKE: Well, no, never.

> *I'm going to do everything men do.*
> *Drink, smoke, tell jokes*
>
> Julie Andrews in *Thoroughly Modern Millie* (1967)

A woman (the wife) in exchange between two men, her husband
and his male friend. But there are always three positions in the
telling of a joke: the person who tells it, the person who listens to
it, the person it is about. So really the wife is in exchange between
five men here, since Jake Gittes tells the story about the wife and
the two men ('this guy' and 'his friend') to his two sidekicks, Duffy
and Walsh.

The pleasure of the dirty joke begins from the child's pleasure
in looking at its sexual organs and those of other people. It is
related to scopophilia, that is, the pleasure in looking (discussed in
next section but one). Pleasure in looking can become the pleasure
of talking about sex, and the dirty joke is a convention which
allows that. In the film Jake Gittes is played by Jack Nicholson and
his performance shows that he enjoys using the words and the
names, simply the saying of 'screw a little bit' (which carries the
unspoken implication that a penis is constantly put into a vagina
and taken out again). Told among men, as it generally is, the dirty
joke gives its teller the fantasy of seducing a woman with the
encouragement of his audience. Like banter, the dirty joke represents a version of masculine style. Jokes work by using a joke
mechanism, a play on words or ideas that temporarily conceals the

meaning. In a simple childish joke it is just a play on words ('When is a door not a door?' 'When it's ajar' = 'a jar') but in more complicated, 'adult' jokes, like this one from *Chinatown*, the play on words leads to something forbidden being said that otherwise could not be spoken. The wife's words, 'You're screwing just like a Chinaman', don't make sense until we reach behind them to the meaning they hide. If she simply and explicitly stated, 'I recognize the sexual techniques you're using because I have been making love with a Chinaman', most of the effect of the joke would be lost because the mechanism of play would have gone. Hence, to explain a joke is to destroy it (and perhaps this joke is one that ought to be destroyed).

In the *Chinatown* joke a play on words allows the men to admit the otherwise unspoken and threatening idea of the wife's adultery. She knows she has been unfaithful but she doesn't say so, and may think her husband doesn't know either. But of course he does know, because *he* has deliberately been making love in a Chinese manner. The husband may get upset by this (the joke doesn't go on to say) but his discomfort is balanced by his superior knowledge – he knows something about his wife that she doesn't know he knows. Has she spoken out deliberately for the satisfaction of saying something he shouldn't understand? Probably not. She speaks spontaneously through sexual excitement because, so the story says, she was 'getting sore as hell'. Thus the joke takes advantage of her submission to passion in contrast to his demonstration of masculine self-control ('he goes out and he smokes a cigarette').

At the price of some jealousy the husband gains a mastery over the wife. But for the teller of the joke, J. J. Gittes, and his audience, Walsh and Duffy, superiority over the wife is offered at no cost. They know that a husband gets 'tired of screwing his wife', they are party to the conversation in which the male friend instructs the husband in the art of Chinese loving, they know the wife has a Chinese lover. She is the butt of the joke, she and her sexual pleasure are passed between the teller of the joke and his assistants as an object in exchange between them. She is exposed to them almost as though they were spectators, watching her in bed with her Chinese lover without her knowing. By means of the joke she is made sexually available to them, a sexual object, an object of knowledge.

This is most obviously the case for Jake, the joke's narrator. Since the teller of a joke has already heard it and found a release of pleasure in it, he can only find new pleasure in it at second hand, as it were, by borrowing it from the listener who is hearing it for the first time. But that is not necessarily so with the dirty joke, nor is it here. Jake comes in from the barber impatient to tell the joke he's just heard and twice brushes aside Duffy's interruption and once Walsh's. In telling it he becomes the man making love to the woman, whether as husband or lover or both. He relives the coitus interruptus, smiling in the film with anticipated pleasure, getting more and more excited as the story gets 'more exciting', finally laughing loudly and orgasmically when he comes to the punchline which reveals both her infidelity and her desire for sexual pleasure.

Jake demands that Walsh and Duffy collaborate with him in making the joke happen, despite their attempted refusals. The telling of the joke is a reassertion of the male bond. So Jake sends Sophie out ('to the little girl's room') while the men talk. He addresses Duffy as 'man', insists that Walsh will 'love this' (the story? the imagined object of the story?), offers the joke as sexual advice to Duffy who's 'always in such a hurry'. The male dirty joke is a particular way of talking about women. In this version of masculinity men are to master women by talking about them and affirming together a male bond which overrides heterosexual desire.

Desire, however, has always got more than one side. In the film *Chinatown* this joke is turned against its teller. It releases various ideas that threaten masculine self-possession. Although the husband is assumed naturally to be tired of screwing his wife, she also is presumably also somewhat tired of her husband. She too has her desires (a Chinese lover because he is exotically other? because they are such dilatory lovers? because there are potentially so many of them?). And she too is capable of deception. The joke only masters such male anxieties by awakening them.

Because the patriarchal system of exchanging women draws attention to the objects exchanged, the feelings towards each other of those who *do* the exchanging have been concealed. Once again masculinity tries to stay invisible. The first three parts of *The Masculine Myth* have described how the male bond works when women are not particularly at issue. The joke from *Chinatown* shows how sublimated male homosexual desire is equally active when the idea of a woman is exchanged between men. This will be so not only for jokes but for all male conversations and writing in which the feminine figures as an object. A good example will occur later on in the article on Warren Beatty, which invites the male reader to share a list of twenty-one women's names.

The *Chinatown* joke also finds another place for male desire. Jake is the only one who laughs at his own joke, the only one who finds pleasure in it. No doubt, in his masculinity, he identifies with the male side of the joke, with the husband, the male friend, the Chinese lover. But in his femininity he must identify with the wife. And, in what is by no means the final twist in the story, the anecdote manages to suggest this also. Just as the wife is constantly interrupted in her love-making, so Jake is constantly interrupted by his two associates while he is telling the joke.

THE MADONNA AND
THE WHORE

'Dynasty', ABC Television, since 1980

Blake Carrington, a self-made man, is an oil tycoon based in Denver, Colorado, and has a fortune estimated at $200 million. In 1954 he married Alexis Morell (Joan Collins) with whom he had three children, Adam, Fallon and Steven. Following her adultery in 1965 they were divorced. Alexis was given a generous financial settlement on condition that she did not visit the children. In 1980 Blake married his secretary, Krystle Jennings (Linda Evans). Accused of manslaughter, also in 1980, he was convicted largely on the testimony of Alexis.

Machinations by Blake's one-time friend, Cecil Colby, led in 1981 to Blake coming close to financial ruin and also to an explosion in which he temporarily lost his sight. In 1982 Alexis married Cecil Colby, who died immediately afterwards leaving her a controlling interest in his company, Colbyco, and instructions to destroy Blake. In the same year Krystle discovered her previous divorce was not valid, nor was her marriage to Blake. Alexis offered her a million dollars to leave Blake for good. However, in 1983 Krystle re-married Blake. In 1985 she had a daughter, Krystina Carrington.

Meanwhile, as chairman of Colbyco, Alexis has become the only woman to succeed in the oil business. In 1984 she persuaded Rashid Ahmed to double-cross Blake in a deal over South China oil, and in consequence Blake lost half his fortune. Alexis has since married Dex Dexter, and rediscovered her long-lost daughter, Amanda.

> *Every woman is a whore except my mother who is a saint*
>
> Italian saying

Out of the tradition of Victorian melodrama, television has developed a genre all of its own, soap opera, a form perfectly adapted to present a sense of the family and the relations between men and women. At present the most popular soap in the world is *Dynasty*. This is watched regularly by one hundred million viewers in more than 70 countries. In Britain it collects an audience of 11 million. It may seem surprising that British television cannot produce glossy, escapist soap opera about immensely rich people and that as a result we have to make do with the mundane realities of *Coronation Street* and *Crossroads*. There is a good reason for this. In a British context the very rich would have to be either aristocratic, lords and ladies, or commoners who had made good. Either way a large chunk of the audience would turn away from them. And that, no doubt, is why, as Rosalind Coward points out in her book *Female Desire*, the story of the Royal Family is the longest-running soap opera in Britain. Only they can appear to be above both class and money.

Alexis and Krystle

The contrast between Alexis and Krystle is at the centre of *Dynasty* and its success. In fact the cover photograph of *Dynasty, the Authorized Biography of the Carringtons* demonstrates this very well. Blake Carrington, in a dinner jacket, stands between Alexis, wearing black, and Krystle, wearing turquoise, while all three look at the camera and the viewer. Blake, therefore, is posed as able to choose between and have at his command both women. They represent the two great types or categories into which women are divided by the masculine myth. The opposition between Krystle and Alexis can be named in all kinds of ways – as Love Sacred and Profane, as Agape and Eros, Platonic love and sexual love, as love versus desire, or, at its crudest, in the American phrase, the difference between 'nice girls' and 'easy lays'.

Together, Krystle and Alexis make up a pair of opposites. Krystle is ash blonde, Alexis brunette. She has blue eyes, Alexis has greeny brown. Krystle's large mouth typically parts into a 'sweet' smile, while Alexis tends to pout and has what the *Authorized Biography* rightly names as 'inviting lips'. Krystle's fringe tends to give her no brow, and so, by implication, little brain; Alexis has a full brow barely covered by curls. The two types are opposed also in terms of sensual and pure, worldly and unworldly and, of

course, work and home. Krystle's name suggests the translucence of crystal while the other has a man's name inside it, Alex-is. The biography unerringly summarizes the difference between them in the appropriate clichés. Krystle is 'an American Aphrodite, good as she is beautiful'. Alexis personifies Kipling's observation that 'the female of the species is deadlier than the male'. Both types relate to a man, Blake Carrington.

The meaning of each stereotype, the 'good girl' and the 'bitch', is repeated and repeated with little change through a long series of events. Basically they are opposed as active to passive. In terms of sexual drive, Alexis says 'yes' and Krystle says 'no'. In terms of narcissism Alexis follows her self-interest while Krystle submits to the interests of others. It is easier to list the men Krystle has turned down than the ones Alexis has made love with. In 1980, when her marriage to Blake was going through a sticky patch,

Krystle was tempted by Matthew Blaisdel but turned him down. In 1981 she didn't even notice Nick Toscanni's passion for her and in 1983 she was again tempted but refused Mark Jennings, who was her first husband.

Alexis seeks to dominate Blake Carrington and her own children in a way that sometimes brings her into conflict with the law. She succeeded in having Blake convicted of manslaughter by testifying in court to his violence, she tried to buy off Krystle. She went along with her son Adam when he tried to poison Jeff Colby and she has schemed with Rashid Ahmed to ruin Blake. Thinking that Kirby Anders, as the daughter of a servant, is not a good enough match for her son Adam, she tells her a family secret that had been kept from her, and Kirby at once leaves. The attempts by Alexis to get rid of Krystle have twice brought the two women to physical violence. It is significant that both occurred only when Krystle felt her maternal interests were being threatened. One fight took place in 1982 at Alexis's studio when Krystle thought Alexis had purposely fired a rifle which scared her horse and caused her miscarriage. The re-match took place, mainly in a lily pond, in 1983, because Krystle thought Alexis was implicated in the departure of her grandson Danny from the Carrington mansion. In these melodramatic scenes the opposition between the two types is vividly dramatized.

The Double Standard
Just as Alexis and Krystle both stand in relation to Blake Carrington, first wife and second, so the two types are a masculine product and projection on to the world of masculine fantasies. As always, for psychoanalysis the difference between the sexes originates in the different paths they follow past the mother. Female heterosexual desire begins with the mother, moves to the father, transfers to the bridegroom; male heterosexual desire begins with the mother and transfers, without any mediating figure, to the bride. This is what lies behind the masculine polarity between the madonna and the whore.

Male sexual feeling has both an affectionate and a sensual side. The affectionate current springs from the little boy's first object, the mother. Later, however, especially at puberty, a second sensual current develops, aimed at an adult woman. However, the second cannot but follow the model for the first. In ideal circumstances, the sensual current will take over from the affectionate one. If it doesn't, or doesn't completely, this is because desire has got stuck or fixated on the first object, the mother. In consequence the man can only desire women who do not recall the incestuous figure forbidden to him. His feeling polarizes between love and desire. In its most acute form this would mean he was impotent with the woman he loved and could only feel sexual desire for other women.

Perhaps the opposition might be so extreme that he could only desire someone who was as far opposed for him to the image of the mother as a prostitute might be. Of those who experience this Freud remarks sadly, 'Where they love they do not desire and where they desire they cannot love.' But he also notes that the condition touches most men in some degree. Its source lies with the proximity between the mother and the bride in the pathway of masculine development. And this goes some way to explain how masculinity tends to approach the feminine in terms of two opposed categories.

But psychoanalysis alone does not go far enough. Other societies, even other patriarchal societies, have interpreted the opposition very differently or hardly felt it at all. Freud himself suggests that the double standard has taken on a much more fierce quality in Western culture since the establishment of Christianity. Whereas the ancient world placed very few barriers on the fulfilment of sexual drive, Christianity made a name for itself by doing just that. The condemnation of sexual desire in Christianity encourages at the same time an idealization of sacred love and precisely the figure of the mother, the Madonna. And the pattern is intensified in bourgeois culture, after the Renaissance. As work and home become ever more separated, culture marks off the woman at home as ever more perfect. She is idealized as wife and mother, in the phrase of the Victorian poet, Coventry Patmore, 'an angel in the house'. The more this saint has to be loved, the more other women will be desired.

Hence the perfect reproduction of a Victorian stereotype in Krystle and Alexis. For all the seeming independence of Alexis, she is not what the *Authorized Biography* calls her, 'a world-class woman who is totally in control of her life'. In fact all her independence and ruthlessness is not for herself but for a man. It is an attempt to regain Blake Carrington in some way. So both she and Krystle are women for men, images in the dominant culture.

As a masculine construction the double standard cuts both ways. It is never unambiguous that Krystle is to be preferred to Alexis. Because she is an object of desire, Alexis is clearly more interesting, more attractive than Krystle, who seems in contrast nice, dull and maternal. Equally, Krystle can be used as a stick to beat Alexis, because in her sexual desire is active and appetitive. The double standard blames women either way and is able to build up considerable amounts of aggression against them – for being both too nice and too desirable, for saying no and for saying yes. As Joan Collins summed it up in an interview recently, 'Alexis is only called a bitch because she's a woman; if a man did what she does, they wouldn't think of it that way.'

THE IDEA OF THE
WOMAN

Down, wanton, down! Have you no shame
That at the whisper of Love's name,
Or Beauty's, presto! up you raise
Your angry head and stand at gaze?

Robert Graves

This section will try to answer the question: why is male heterosexual desire presented as absolute and undifferentiating, as though it were always the same, no matter what the time, the place, or for that matter the person? In the dominant view women's desire is shown as directed towards a particular person, and usually, as in the romantic novels of Mills and Boon, discreet dots fill the place of the sexual act. Masculinity, however, is constructed on all sides as above all an insatiable sexual appetite, something that seeks satisfaction everywhere – in posters, magazines, advertising, soft- and hard-core pornography – in images of women or bits of women.

For the dominant culture itself this is all a non-question. Male sexual feeling *is* a bodily appetite, a matter of biological instinct not drive. And so the penis fills with blood 'at the whisper of Love's name' because it cannot *not* do so, just as saliva comes to the tongue at the sight of food. This is of course nonsense. Even if there is a biological difference between male and female sexual instinct, it would still have to be taken up, interpreted and a construction put upon it according to the operation of a particular human culture. An earlier section gave a vivid illustration of that. Whereas images of the phallus were commonplace in ancient society, they have not been so in our society since the advent of Christian hegemony. This was bound to make a difference to masculine sexuality. And in any case the distinction between instinct and drive means that sexuality cannot be separated from the symbolic forms in which it takes on representation.

For both these reasons the idea that male heterosexual desire is a natural force has to be rejected. And so the question is why contemporary culture wishes to think of masculinity that way. What organization of drives will explain the dominant idea that masculine desire is abstract, universal and inescapable, that it is always provoked as a kind of automatic reflex to the idea of Woman? It is supposed to be as obvious and direct as the image of women embodied by the famous Monroe Calendar. There she is, so there it is. All I have to do is look. Down, wanton, down.

'Here's looking at you, kid'

The idea of male desire as a universal imperative corresponds to the equally generalized and abstract representation of woman as Woman. And this has a very clear cultural and historical background, as John Berger suggests in his book *Ways of Seeing*. A number of quite separate innovations at the time of the Renaissance, including the development of a market for paintings, the system of linear perspective able to give a realistic effect, and the use of oil paint, were brought together. The result was a means of producing an image of a naked woman vividly and in graphic detail. It was rapidly promoted into the tradition of painting female nudes. But it should not be forgotten that for every painting of a naked woman there was a male purchaser. The idea of Woman supposes an equally abstract version of masculine desire.

From the high cultural fine-art tradition the representation of woman as an object to be looked at spreads in the nineteenth century into music-hall, engraving and finally photography. To these the twentieth century adds film and television, as well as cheap methods of colour reproduction. The high cultural presentation of woman as an object for male gaze extends until it can encompass the calendar, 'Golden Dreams', on the wall of a million garages. Monroe in 1949 is portrayed in almost exactly the same way as the reclining nude in Titian's *Venus of Urbino* in 1576. Each presumes very much the same conception of masculine looking and masculine desire. Wanting is as much a matter of immediate recognition as sight.

In a brilliant and original essay, reprinted in *Popular Television and Film*, Laura Mulvey has analysed this tradition of pleasure in looking as a form of scopophilia. In doing so she has emphasized its patriarchal content, that it brings about an unequal relation between male and female in which woman is to be an image and man a bearer of the look. Not unnaturally, she concentrates on the way the cultural system affects ideas of women, and though her account draws on psychoanalysis, it is not particularly concerned with asking how the system offers a version of masculinity.

Scopophilia has to be understood as the combination of three terms from three oppositions: masculine/feminine; active/passive; sexual desire/narcissism. Scopophilia begins with the child's pleasure in looking at its own genitals, and develops into the pleasure of looking at the genitals of other people ('You show me yours and I'll show you mine'). Thus it develops from being a narcissistic way of loving yourself into something mainly sexual. It also divides into active and passive, active being the pleasure of looking at others, or voyeurism, passive being the pleasure of being looked at, or exhibitionism. Within the dominant culture these oppositions become mapped on to gender. Photographs treat looking at women as active and masculine and show women as passive objects to be looked at. This generalization can be tested against the thirty or so photographs in any day's issue of a popular newspaper. Once this regime of looking has lined up active with masculine and passive with feminine, it is then able to distribute sexual desire and narcissism into two categories. Men are invited to desire women by actively looking at images of them, women to identify with the images passively looked at.

In the calendar photograph Monroe is styled as an object to be looked at. She is posed in a fixed position, twisting sideways so that the male viewer can get as close as possible to seeing her from all sides at once, and as though she was simultaneously upright and lying down. Her head, half-hidden behind her arm, is turned sharply to the viewer so that the muscle of her neck is rigid with the effort. And the look in her eyes is precisely the look of the woman being looked at and submitting to male inspection. Colour photography and lighting combine to treat her body as a kind of landscape which the male gaze may explore in all its perfect, contoured detail.

So strong is this cultural regime of looking that it resists simple subversion. Attempts to attack it by reversing images don't seem to come off, as some experiments have shown. If a man is posed, lit and photographed in the same kind of way as the Monroe Calendar, the result is often comic, or grotesque, or reveals an attractive femininity in the male image. There is, however, another way of

The Sun, 16 September 1985

approaching the issue, which works if the distinction between sexual desire and narcissism is kept in mind. The cultural tradition of scopophilia tries to assign them into hard and fast categories, keeping desire for active male looking and self-love for women's identification with what is looked at. They can never be separated as easily, as the football pages of the popular press may prove.

For a decade *The Sun* newspaper has carried a photograph on page three of an almost naked woman, its 'Page Three Girl'. Clearly, according to the cultural tradition of scopophilia, the male viewer is expected to desire the woman sexually and not identify with her. However, the situation is reversed in the back pages of *The Sun*, in the football pages. These contain photographs of partly clothed young men displaying themselves. Now obviously the official intention is to offer these bodies to the male viewer for identification. They are always active, footballers in movement, and their look rarely engages the viewer's. But even if they are active and not in a still pose, they are fixed once and for all in the frozen moment of a photograph. They are therefore open to active scopophilic looking, and the weight of the tradition must encourage this. No matter how much it is disavowed, these photographs of handsome youths with flashing thighs must represent objects of desire for male readers of *The Sun*.

This suggestion throws the whole dominant system for picturing men and women into crisis. For the system depends on lining up three sets of opposed terms (active/passive, masculine/feminine, desire/narcissism), so that active looking is lined up with masculinity and sexual desire, passive being with femininity and identification. In practice desire and narcissism always interact, and so, if the thesis of bisexuality is correct, do masculine and feminine in a given individual. How can the imposed regime ever prevent the feminine side of a male viewer from *identifying* with Marilyn Monroe? How can it stop the male viewer from *desiring* the male object in an image?

Masculine Desire and the Essence of Woman

What needs to be explained is the way masculine desire seems to take the form of a categorical imperative both when it comes to looking at women and looking at images of women. Scopophilia combines at least three mechanisms: narcissism, idealization and fetishism.

Although scopophilia activates desire, it also works with a strong element of narcissism in the form of a wish to master. In this respect looking at images of women is a function of the masculine ego, its need to keep everything under surveillance, see perfectly, dominate through vision. The mastery of the masculine ego, as was suggested earlier, requires a threat in order to be exercised, just as the idea of the unified body depends on the idea of the body in pieces. This notion is particularly relevant to scopophilia and masculine desire, for they are focused on the idea of a woman's naked body.

A photographic image of a naked body excites the masculine ego because it both poses and resolves a threat. Thus, the real body is lacking, is absent, and that is a threat, but a threat apparently mastered at a glance because the image of what is missing is so palpably present. Marilyn Monroe died in 1960 but here, in 1986, the photographic sign of her is still very much alive, or so it seems. This pleasurable sense of mastery can come from a painting but it is enormously increased by photography, which can give a much greater effect of realism.

An image of a naked woman poses a threat for mastery in another way, that is, as a sexual threat. The feminine, felt as other than masculine, is a threat to masculinity, and an image of a naked woman is even more demonstrably a threat since it is the more manifestly feminine. But perfect clarity of vision promises to fix this threat. Since it will never go away, at least it can be known in every detail so you can keep an eye on it. And this effect is combined with another by which the masculine ego seeks mastery. Instead of all the different women in the world, the image of Monroe offers to sum them all up into one. Although she seems so real – for what could be more real than the naked body? – she is in fact an ideal. This is *the* perfect female body, *the* object of desire, *the* Woman. If the ego is faced with a summing up, an abstraction, the essence, then all the others can be safely ignored.

Idealization of the Woman acts for the masculine ego but also for masculine desire. As was discussed in the last section, such desire must try to reconcile two feelings, affection and sensuality, love and lust. One derives from the figure of the mother, the other from that of the bride, though of course for masculinity the two figures always risk occurring in dangerous confusion. The perfected image of the perfect female nude seems to reconcile them. For on the one hand it is a perfect ideal, as was the mother. But on the other it is an indelibly sexual image which no one could possibly confuse with the mother. Masculine heterosexual desire, as focused in images of naked women, brings together a quality of desire and an object of desire. The quality comes from the mother, desire in the form of a universal imperative. But the object comes from the bride, since what is desired is another adult woman.

A third strand in the mix is introduced by fetishism, something that has already been mentioned in connection with the clarity of masculine style. Masculinity, in this account, is always liable to find the threat of castration in an image of a woman's body. This will be so even with the Monroe Calendar in which she has her legs discreetly closed and tucked up underneath her. It will be more demonstrably a threat in the imagery of hard-core pornography which displays female genitals. But the more intense the threat, the more complete the fetishistic response. Two things in images of women become obviously fetishized. One is the woman's body itself, which can appear to have the firmness, solidity and unity of the phallus for which it is a fetishistic substitute. The other is the pleasure of looking, which, with all the techniques of modern colour photography, has come to seem ever more vivid, substantial and complete. If this sounds surprising, it should be remembered that the unfortunate young man who came to Freud about his problems had made a fetish not simply of a shine on the nose but of a *glance* at the nose.

In a complex organization, all these elements work together in the dominant culture to produce masculine heterosexual desire as an ungovernable force. Such desire is defined culturally in an imbalanced equation between active and male, passive and female. It is defined further by a particular relation to narcissism, idealization and fetishism. If the feminine is treated as an essence, the Woman, masculine desire must take a corresponding form. Hence, the verse from Robert Graves's poem is exactly accurate. It is the abstract and general form of femininity as 'Love', as 'Beauty' which provokes a similarly generalized expression of male desire.

BEING IN LOVE

'Love on Your Side' by the Thompson Twins (1982)

(1) I hear you laughing in some other room,
and it makes me feel locked out
You say my passion often stifles you
and you need to move about.
Well I was told that boys need girls and girls need boys,
you say that's not true.
You would rather fool around than be alone with me,
well that's alright for you.

Chorus
'Cause you've got love, love, love on your side,
yes you've got love, love, love on your side,
yes you've got love, love, love on your side,
yes you've got love, love, love on your side.

(2) I brought you sentimental roses,
but you gave them all away
I played you all my favourite records,
Then we spent the night in talking, talking all the time,
you sent me home.
I was so surprised to find that after all
it doesn't hurt to be alone.

Chorus

Words and music by Tom Bailey, Joe Leeway and Alannah Currie
copyright © 1982 by Point Music/ATV Music

You are everything and everything is you

Old song

The world of popular music is a special enclave in the dominant culture. Within it masculinity is imagined almost as the exact opposite of what it is supposed to be elsewhere. In the poetry of these songs men cry, moan, sob, sigh, ache and suffer. They address women as 'baby' and expect to be addressed as 'baby' in return. It is as though everything repressed by the dominant image of the masculine ego – hard, firm, self-possessed, watchfully defensive – is here expressed in excess.

Sales of records in Britain have declined recently from their 1978 peak, a year when 86 million albums and 89 million singles were marketed. This is truly a dominant and dominating culture. Language and attitudes from pop songs permeate our waking life. At breakfast, at work, in pubs, the cinema, television, parties, they try to keep the values of home and the personal alive even in the impersonal environment of work. The music endlessly recycles simple variations of the same kind of melody and harmony familiar to us from, for example, the Church of England's *Hymns Ancient and Modern*. It is often supposed that only the music matters and the words don't. But if this were so, there would only be instrumentals and the record companies would save themselves the money spent on singers and songwriters. Even if the words are inaudible at first hearing, they penetrate through repetition to a level beneath conscious awareness.

Words tell and retell very much the same story of unhappy adolescent love. It is as though a whole culture were stuck with a moment of development after childhood but before the social responsibilities of adult life. This is, to borrow a phrase, the heart of a heartless world. Many songs are unisex, in the sense that they can just as well be sung by a man or a woman. And there is a reason for this. Love, romantic love, being in love is a form of mutual narcissism. So, if its model is a kind of closed circle, 'I love you because you love me', then it is likely the songs will express a reciprocated feeling and be sung equally by male and female singers.

But it is not possible for two people to stand in exactly the same place. Similarly the circle of narcissism can never be closed because you can never really see and love me from the position I see and love you. The theme of unhappy and unrequited love, you don't love me as I love you, tries to make up for this. And the break in the circle admits an imbalance or inequality between the idea of the masculine and the idea of the feminine put forward in the songs. Within an apparently shared world, masculinity finds a privileged voice, and one that is surprisingly traditional, as it is in Tom Bailey's version of 'Love on Your Side'.

Romantic or courtly love is a thousand years old and seems unique to Western culture. It was unknown in the ancient world of Greece and Rome. The idea that a personal relationship between a man and a woman could lift them into a transcendent dimension, a spiritual paradise like that of the Christian paradise, was a novelty introduced in the South of France at the end of the eleventh century. In the lyrics of the troubadour poets of that period the woman who is loved is treated as a superior being, addressed as 'my lady', sometimes even as 'my lord'. Despite appearances, the treatment works to the man's advantage. The Woman is put on a pedestal and worshipped so she can be kept in place. Up there she cannot move.

The lyrics of 'Love on Your Side' reproduce once again this old relation. She is the mistress, he is her loyal servant, constant in love despite her independence, indifference or superiority. Despite his seeming servility, he gets the pay-off that he can only be seen as she would see him from her idealized position. Whatever she may feel and want, he can insist on it working his way. It is bigger than both of them, or so he says.

In the lyrics of 'Love on Your Side' her independence is constantly overwhelmed by his love and what it compels her to be. Her 'laughing' makes him feel 'locked out', she wants to 'move' but his 'passion' tries to stop her. He insists that sexual feeling is a kind of natural instinct that makes men and women complements of each other, but she refuses this and wants something beyond his masculine desire. He wants her to himself, to 'be alone', while she wants to be with others. One might think this was quite enough to terminate the affair. But in the passionate repetitions of the chorus all is swept aside. Her independence, her rejection of him is made over into something else. Her superiority is 'alright', in fact just what he really wants. If she looks down on him, he can be seen as he wants to be seen. She has become his mirror, reflecting him as the perfect lover, wholly given over to passion. She has love on her side, whether she wants it or not.

The more she hurts him, the more superior she becomes and the more his role as lover is confirmed. Like the true courtly or romantic lover he brings her 'sentimental roses'. It is an act which strongly marks the singer as masculine for it is a line which in present culture could not yet be sung plausibly by a woman. Unlike a troubadour, and like a modern lover, he doesn't sing to her but plays her his records. They talk instead of making love and she sends him home. The relation of master and slave, or here mistress and servant, is inherently aggressive. Because she is treated as superior, this masks his aggressive attempt to hold her in the position he – and love – imposes. And the aggression starts to emerge in the lyrics when he leaves and begins to find he can do without her. In fact, however, the third verse of the lyrics, which has not been quoted here, does not follow this traditional path. Partly because the song has explored the traditional roots of romantic love, the last verse begins to explore his uncertainty and a recognition that the rules of love are changing.

This song has been chosen because it shows clearly, perhaps in an extreme form, the basic structure of being in love. It is at root a masculine idea, a position offered for masculinity in the dominant culture. Although elsewhere being in love may presuppose more balance between the partners, it nevertheless repeats the version of masculine mastery concealed inside the male lover's seeming subservience. To have love on your side means that the beloved *must* reflect the lover's image of himself.

Torvill and Dean are a pair of ice-skating champions who came to prominence in 1984. In their most famous routine, danced to the music of Ravel's 'Bolero', he takes the role of a bullfighter and she is his cape. After a number of movements which recall the passes made by the toreador over the bull, the cape is discarded. The climax leaves Jayne Torvill prone on the ice at the feet of Christopher Dean. The position of the two figures in the publicity

for their 1985 World Tour repeats the traditional stereotype of romantic love, showing how masculinity is imagined in relation to femininity.

He is the master, she is the servant. He is physically active, turning, lifting, straining, while she is posed, arms akimbo, as a passive object. Her look, from underneath veiled lids, is abstract and unfocused. He, however, is looking at her, so that she is the object of his gaze. The vacant look in her eyes makes them a kind of mirror in which he may imagine himself reflected.

At the same time the pose suggests something else. In English the word 'thing' has meant and can mean the phallus, and she is his thing in this sense. The relative positioning of the two figures corresponds exactly to the schema previously discussed, the distinction between being and having the phallus. She is supported and held by him almost as though she were a baby dandled on daddy's knee. Fixed and passive, she is posed to *be* the phallus. In the pose her body rises upright in front of him from the level of the hips. In having her, he *has* the phallus.

Love as a Masculine Idea: Idealization, Narcissism, Phallicism

As suggested already, the tradition of romantic love stretches back to the courtly love of the feudal period. Arguably, in terms of the importance it attributes to individuals, it is one of the main ways bourgeois culture is conceived in the womb of feudalism. Certainly after the Renaissance, it loses its courtly garb and becomes, in principle, democratically available to all. As a cultural form it is transmitted above all in the poetry of the high cultural tradition, by Shakespeare, Donne, and the English Romantic poets. In the twentieth century, through the songs of popular culture, it imposes itself throughout Western culture. Psychoanalysis would understand this tradition of 'being in love' especially in terms of three features: idealization; narcissism; phallicism. It also confirms that love is an exercise of masculinity.

The analysis of being in love begins by noticing that love is invariably unhappy. It revolves around disappointment, pain, loss, a sense of being abandoned, as in the Thompson Twins' song, where the sound of her laughing with her friends makes him feel left out. In this respect love is close to melancholy, though neither can be grasped without some understanding of the nature of the 'I'.

People often say things like, 'I really think I oughtn't do this.' In that kind of sentence there are clearly two 'I's, an 'I' which does it and another 'I' which is critical of the first one. One is the ego, the other the superego, the voice of conscience. The superego develops out of self-love, initially as a sense of the former self, then of that as a better self, which then becomes like the voice of my parents and finally turns into the voice of social authority. Melancholy and being in love are close kin because it is possible to set up an object, particularly a love object, in the place of either the ego or the superego.

Mourning, typically for the death of a loved one, works itself out in the course of time. Melancholy doesn't. Melancholy, like that of, say, Hamlet after the death of his father, is mourning which has got stuck. Or it is like the famous Widow of Windsor, Queen Victoria, who spent the last forty years of her life in seclusion doing little else but regret the death of her husband in 1861. If she was a typical melancholic her thoughts must have taken the form of constant reproaches for some imagined responsibility for his death. Psychoanalysis would explain the process by saying she had kept him alive, as it were, by putting him in the place of her ego. But the price for this is that her own self speaks in the accents of the superego, constantly reproaching the ego and criticizing it.

Being in love is the same process with the positions reversed. The loved object becomes internalized but this time it is set up in the superego. The loved one begins to take on all the authority of the voice of conscience. She – if it is a she – has more than love on her side, for she has morality as well. She becomes the lover's morality, and whatever she does is good and right. But the price now is the impoverishment of the ego. His abasement guarantees her perfection – or at least that is how he wishes to regard the situation.

Freud states explicitly that men have been more prone to over-valuing or idealizing a woman in this way. The reason is the usual one. Idealization begins when the child thinks its parents are perfect. If the masculine individual is more liable to idealize a love object, it is because the image of the mother trenches so much more immediately on to the image of the bride. Idealization, seeing someone as transcendentally perfect, is yet another way in which male heterosexuality may hope to re-find love for the mother in an adult object of desire, The (Perfect) Woman.

This typically masculine idealization co-operates with the masculine ego. In an old image in seventeenth-century poetry the male lover wishes to be so close to his lady that he may see himself reflected in her eyes. No one can ever see themselves from the same point of view as they are seeing. The 'I' or 'eye' that looks at me in a mirror is not me but an image produced according to the laws of optics. But love seems to come close to seeing yourself seeing yourself. You can imagine that another person looks at you in the way you'd like to see yourself. And even if they don't, or don't perfectly, others can see you in the way you want, as the perfect lover.

Being in love is thus another version of the mastery of the masculine ego. All of the rest of the world, everything that is not the self, can be gathered together into a single point, the eyes of The Woman. Fixed there, it can appear as though mastered, known, perfectly visible once and for all. The effect is like that celebrated in the old song, 'Everything is you and you are everything'.

Being in love offers the fantasy that the masculine ego should see itself in what is most other than it. The essence of Man seems to find unity and mastery in relation to the essence of Woman. Two moves are required to make the effect plausible, yet both are impossible and the structure collapses. The first move reduces the varied forms of desire – male and female, homosexual and heterosexual – to an essence. It tries to turn 'everything' into a 'you' where 'I' recognize myself. Secondly, the organization of being in love tries to make these two essences of Man and Woman complements of each other when they are in fact different. What actually emerges is, as usual, that her essence and her desire is the complement of his – that is, subordinate. This can be understood clearly enough if being in love is considered in terms of the phallic system.

Love and the Phallus

In the dominant culture the scenario of love, male narcissism as would-be master of what is other than itself, can be played out in terms of being and having the phallus. For several years now an advertisement for Dormeuil Men's Clothing has appeared in the *Sunday Times* magazine section. It invariably shows a woman with an abstracted look posed in a fixed position alongside a man wearing a suit and looking at the camera. In one particular image, which appeared in 1981, the woman was placed literally on a pedestal from which she could not move. Her pose was almost perfectly upright and she wore a clinging red dress which, with her long, loose hair filling the space between head and shoulders, made her figure a single unity. Her look was unfixed, either an inward gaze or a vacant stare into space. Her passivity made her figure able to serve as a phallic object, to be the phallus.

Meanwhile the man in the suit stood resting his right elbow on top of her plinth. His left arm and hand were poised at the buttons of his coat just below the midriff, over the point where the threat of castration would be focused. His right hand and arm were raised erect in exact parallel to her body. He directed a hard, firm, controlling gaze straight at the camera and the viewer. Through the placing of his arms, what she is has been made over into what he has. He has the phallus because she is the phallus for him.

The image was a kind of epitome. It brilliantly sums up in a single photograph the abstract schema of the phallic system. This assumes two things. Firstly, it presumes that the difference between the sexes – sexual difference – consists of her difference *from* him (his masculinity supposedly is normal and universal). If the feminine is seen as different, other than masculine, it shows what masculinity lacks and so represents the threat of castration for him. But in the scheme of love, threat and solace are brought together. She opens up a gap that can seem closed if she keeps perfectly still. The wound she makes can be staunched if she remains fixed, uplifted and inert, for in this pose she becomes the phallus. Masculinity can be represented as active in having the phallus on condition that the feminine is passive in being the phallus.

Secondly, as noted before, the schema comes unstuck with the admission of male homosexual desire. It relies on a strict distribution of male narcissism and desire – the woman is there to be looked at sexually, the sleek male to be identified with. But the divided nature of male sexuality means that this distribution cannot be relied on.

FAME, WEALTH, AND THE LOVE OF WOMEN

Beatty kisses but won't tell

by Lesley Salisbury in Hollywood

Certainly, it's hard to take your eyes off Warren Beatty when he arrives at a party, but it's worth it, just to see everyone else's reaction. Men watch him out of the corner of their eyes, subconsciously straightening their ties – or, if you're in Hollywood, their gold chains – trying to fathom the appeal of this short-sighted, rumple-suited sex symbol as he squints his way round the room.

Women tend to react in three predictable ways. There's the 'let's pretend to ignore him' gambit, which is really an attempt to attract his interest; the casual move towards him so that he can't turn round without bumping into a pliant elbow or hip; or the direct approach: 'Warren, darling, it's been *ages*, we *must* have lunch,' and a flutter of phone numbers – most of them, no doubt, already in his little black book.

TV Times, 29 June 1985

Writing of the artist, whom he assumes is invariably male, Freud tells a kind of parable. The artist is a man obsessed with fantasies of masculine success, summed up as the wish for wealth, fame and the love of women. Through his special ability as an artist, he is able to translate these into an artistic form, where they become available to others without shame or embarrassment as marketable products. He thus gets in fact what he once only had in fantasy – wealth, fame and the love of women.

The little story hints at the problem the male artist faces once he has been successful. For now that he has got what he really wanted he does not need to fantasize. He has the problem of going on to new success, doing it again. The account does not confront its own assumption that the artist is working in a capitalist economy in which art is a saleable commodity. Nor does it question at all the fact that this idea of the male artist conforms to the dominant myth of masculinity. Much better than the businessman, the politician or the general, the figure of the artist can embody such masculine fantasy. Whether as writer or actor or media personality, the artist appears to be after something of human value, art, so that power and recognition are mere adjuncts to his art. And so also, in the prevailing fantasy, are women.

We do not know what Warren Beatty is really like and in fact the article quotes him as saying, 'I am nothing like what you read.' However, in what we read he becomes a definite image for masculine fantasy. The article is written from a woman's point of view and assigns very clear positions to its male and female readers. Although it is frequently facetious about the figure of Beatty, it offers women a position of identification with the writer of the article. As the second paragraph says, other women try unsuccessfully to arrange a rendezvous with him, but the reader, in fantasy identification with the author of the piece, meets Beatty over lunch, as she later describes. Meanwhile the male reader is allowed to imagine himself as Warren Beatty.

This is a position of mastery, and as always, vision is part of its effect. It is said to be 'hard to take your eyes off Warren Beatty', and, as well as photographs, the article includes careful description of his bodily presence, height, weight and looks. He has been 'in the public eye all these years'. But his fame and the recognition accorded to him does not make him simply an object. He is presented as a mastering subject. Of the 'predictable ways' in which women try to catch his attention it is said that 'He's seen them all'. And further down, with reference to his many love affairs, his sister Shirley MacLaine is reported as saying he has his 'master's degree in ladykilling'.

Because his life seems to be devoted to the non-commercial end of art, Beatty's power and ownership of capital can be presented as mere adjuncts to his mastery. Casual and apparently incidental references are slipped in to his 'Hollywood Hills home' and his 'personal fortune'. In terms of the phallic system he possesses the phallus. Men look at him surreptitiously, 'straightening their ties', their own less adequate emblems of male power.

For this figure of masculine fantasy, women are treated as mere adjuncts, a bagatelle. The headline – 'BEATTY KISSES BUT WON'T TELL' – links him to a nursery rhyme character:

> Georgie Porgie, pudding and pie,
> Kissed the girls and made them cry;
> When the boys came out to play,
> Georgie Porgie ran away.

Opposite a nearly full-page photograph of Beatty smiling like a cat who has got the cream and waving in acknowledgement, the article prints small inset photographs of six women with the caption, 'Warren's women'. It also manages to reveal along the way the names of a further fifteen of what it refers to, twice, as 'his women'. Like the imaginary first father, Beatty has all the women to himself.

His heterosexual desire is presented as a form of natural instinct, and he is written of as a stallion among mares, a 'shallow superstud'. But the nature of his desire is contradictory. He is said to be an 'insatiable lover' who made love 'four or five times a day, even while he was on the phone'. Shirley MacLaine comments that 'Sex is the most important thing in his life' but it is also of very little importance if he makes love even while on the phone. Women are important only as supports for his masculine ego, objects to reflect his narcissism, part of his desire for power and recognition.

Casanova, Don Juan and Homosexual Desire

There are three fairly obvious ways to understand what drives this figure of masculine fantasy, and no doubt each is present to some extent in any one example, as it is here. The Casanova figure is trapped by the double standard, searching endlessly for the mother in one passionate affair after another. But where he loves he cannot desire and where he desires he cannot love. The woman seduced is immediately discarded as the search goes on. In the article Beatty is rumoured to have proposed marriage to only one woman, who turned him down.

The Don Juan figure makes love promiscuously because he hates his lovers. To him they represent sexual difference, and so the threat of castration. And so they are to be destroyed. This underlies a reference in the article to Beatty's 'ladykilling'. A third motive is the attempt to deny homosexual desire. The article brings this out when it identifies Beatty with the hero of the film *Shampoo*, in which he plays a Beverly Hills hairdresser 'mincing convincingly to disarm suspicious husbands' while making love with their wives.

But there is another, more significant way in which the embodiment of fame, wealth and the love of women rests on male homosexual desire. In naming 'Warren's women', the piece from the *TV Times* treats the feminine as simply dependent on masculinity, and offers positions to men and women readers accordingly. For the male reader, the list of names becomes an object in exchange between himself and the represented hero. Homosexual desire in the form of their male bond is given a covert importance that pushes heterosexual desire to the margins. If Beatty makes love while on the telephone it is because he is telling a male friend about it, and in this article the male reader is offered that position. The effect is strengthened because the report is written for us in the way it is from a woman's point of view. In thinking only about Warren Beatty and making so much of meeting him for lunch she places herself in the position of one of 'Warren's women' and invites the female reader to see herself in this role.

Each of these previous sections on the masculine and the feminine has considered the way the phallic system tries to enforce itself in different areas of the dominant culture. Each has examined how the masculine myth aims to deny the feminine, both by holding it on to the masculine ego and containing it through the male bond. The final two sections turn to more sinister and deeply wrought effects of the myth, in terms of male jealousy and how the feminine itself may figure as a bad object for masculinity, an object for the death drive.

JEALOUSY

Harry Moseby and Ellen in 'Night Moves'
directed by Arthur Penn (1975)

A footballer who is now a private detective in Los Angeles, Harry Moseby specializes in divorce cases and watching people committing adultery. He is married to Ellen, who works as an antique dealer. At one point in the film she tells him she is going to the cinema with a friend, Charles, while Harry works on a case. Passing the cinema later he sees her come out with Charles and another man. Charles leaves and Ellen goes off with the other man. When their car stops at some lights Harry watches her lean across in the car to kiss the man. When she comes home she tells him that after the movie she and Charles had gone on to eat.

Having noted the number of the other man's car, Harry visits him in his apartment by the sea. It is beautifully furnished with walls lined by fine pictures. The man, Marty Heller, has blue eyes, wears blue jeans and a blue shirt, and walks with a stick. Harry says he saw them coming out of the movie and threatens to become aggressive. When he confronts Ellen she asks why he didn't come to her first and he says, 'I wanted to see what he looked like.' He says that if he'd not known for certain who the man was, she would have lied, passing him off as 'some faggot friend of Charles'. Divorce is in the air. The film then moves back to its main narrative.

Ev'ry breath you take
ev'ry move you make
ev'ry bond you break
ev'ry step you take
I'll be watching you

'Every breath you take' by Sting,
reproduced by kind permission of Virgin Music
(Publishers) Ltd

Although male jealousy has been represented in our culture, it is much more rarely portrayed in popular culture today. There may be two separate reasons for this. One is that male jealousy is very likely to disrupt the masculine myth. This, I think, is why the myth has often stepped around male jealousy, as it does for example when a man is presented as seemingly unaware of and disavowing his partner's attachment to other men. Another reason is that the traditional version through which the myth handles jealousy seems to have been rendered implausible today.

It runs like this. Told by an envious friend that his wife was committing adultery, the husband would rapidly and successfully ascertain the truth of the allegation. Thereupon he would first confront the erring woman, reducing her to shame and tears by the force of his moral denunciation. He would then seek out her lover, challenge him to a duel or match him at fisticuffs, and mete out the punishment he deserved. After retiring to get drunk with male friends and find solace in the male bond, he would return to a suitably repentant wife, after which her lapse would be forgotten.

Something like this is hinted at in *Night Moves*. Harry does make certain that his jealous suspicion is true, and he does confront his wife, though only after seeing Marty Heller. But when he does face Marty in his house, he cannot possibly respond to his sneering 'Why don't you take a swing at me?' Marty is older than him, limps, and uses a walking stick. The date on the calendar is 1974, not 1874. The masculine myth no longer has the confidence to occupy the territory of jealousy, even though it is extremely important. The reason is partly that the myth is under attack in this area, partly that male jealousy is always liable to undermine the myth, as happens in *Night Moves*.

Psychoanalysis has a very straightforward account of male jealousy, one that integrates a number of features already considered. Jealousy has three layers, distinguished as competitive or normal jealousy, projected jealousy, and delusional jealousy. Yet all three are present to some degree in any one instance of male jealousy. Competitive jealousy derives from a man's incestuous feeling for his mother. Thus, the other man in the triangle is seen to be in the position of the father and the woman as the mother, so that her attachment to the other man is felt as the mother's betrayal. In projected jealousy, as the name suggests, the man's own desire for infidelity is projected on to the woman.

Neither competitive – so-called 'normal' jealousy – nor the projected kind can be properly understood apart from the culture in which they occur. Patriarchy, based as it is on the exchange of women, will help to intensify male jealousy if women are supposed to be dependent on men, wives on husbands. And bourgeois culture also will turn the screw tighter if wives are valued as commodities and idealized as the heart of a heartless world. In the film, Harry Moseby's jealousy of Ellen has a social aspect. Her work in the art world gives her a social status above him, a former football player. And there is a suggestion that he is financially dependent on her earnings.

In delusional jealousy a man imagines his partner's infidelity even when there is no actual cause. He watches her all the time, interpreting minute details of her behaviour as signs of love for another man. It is, in this respect, like the paranoia which shows itself in fantasies of being persecuted, and for psychoanalysis the origin is the same – defence against homosexuality. It can be stated as a formula, '*I* do not love him, *she* loves him'. Although these three kinds of male jealousy can be distinguished from each other, Freud emphasizes that each of the three components occurs with the others in some degree. Even if delusional jealousy invents what is not a real situation, the line between real and imaginary is hard to draw in the other cases. Especially in an officially monogamous society, people will feel the impulse to love more than one person even if the impulse is not always followed.

Harry Moseby's jealousy has a basis in fact – Ellen is making love with Marty Heller. There is an element of competitive jealousy in Harry so that he feels as though the mother is betraying him with the father. Ellen sometimes looks and acts in a maternal way to him, while the other man seems older than him and walks with a stick. Projected jealousy is certainly present, for Harry does desire other women and later in the narrative commits adultery while in Florida. But what the movie shows particularly strongly is a component of delusional jealousy.

Harry's chosen profession as a private eye means that he spends his time keeping men and women under surveillance. Cruising the dark streets in his car he is constantly looking and watching, seeing but unseen. Going to the Magnolia cinema on impulse he catches sight of his wife going off with Marty Heller. He scans the scene for minute particulars, following their car, gazing with the sick look of the jealous man as Ellen kisses Marty by the traffic lights. Just as she appears to have turned against him, so does his professional expertise as a detective. His masculine pleasure in knowing about other people's adulterous affairs is reversed when it is his own wife he is spying on. He memorizes the car number.

Later, at home, when she comes back, he has the unpleasant pleasure of knowing she is lying to him. Charles left and she did not go to eat with him. Because this is realist cinema we as viewers are forced to share Harry's visual mastery, watching exactly as he watches, though of course our pleasure is a safe one. We know he is only a character in a fiction.

The figure of Marty Heller is lent a connotation of bisexuality because of his association with art and the aesthetic in contrast to Harry's athleticism. Harry (played by Gene Hackman) stands awkwardly among Heller's paintings, looking at the blue sea and the man dressed all in blue. His homosexual desire is expressed later when he tells Ellen, 'I wanted to see what he looked like', and again when he speaks of him as 'some faggot friend of Charles'. Harry insists that Ellen loves Marty so as to defend himself against the possibility that he might love him.

Jealousy and Masculinity

Male jealousy is almost unspeakable. It is so powerful because it sets in motion many features of the masculine myth while at the same time comprehensively undermining it. When Harry watches his wife put her arm round Marty's neck and bend over to kiss him, the look that comes to his face combines disgust and a kind of shame, as though at his own complicity. He encounters the loss of most of what his masculinity claims for itself.

Jealousy activates the full resources of the masculine ego. Vigilance, knowledge, visual mastery are all called into play, but mastery is turned inside out, as it is when Harry finds it is his own wife he is spying on. Jealousy is the 'green-eyed monster' because it paints the world it sees the colour of bile. If it is not disavowed, it poses a threat which becomes worse, not better, through knowledge.

The dominant idea of the relation between the masculine and the feminine is challenged at every point. Instead of women being objects of exchange, jealousy reveals them as agents, subjects, able to do the exchanging themselves. The confident teller of jokes becomes their butt. His former madonna turns into the whore, moving out of her fixed place as his love ideal to somewhere else. Scopophilic pleasure in looking becomes the unpleasurable means of knowing what he doesn't want to know.

Jealousy wholly disrupts the male bond, in two ways at once. First of all, the potentially companionable male friend is revealed as a traitor and an enemy. But secondly, more seriously, the basis of the male bond in homosexual desire is uncovered. Jealousy expresses desire that has been repressed rather than sublimated. Thus it acts to destroy the foundation of the masculine myth, by revealing that masculinity can never exist in a pure state, masculine all the way through. And in so doing it is more than likely to cast the feminine in the most terrible role the myth provides for her, as bad object. Discussion of this has been reserved for the final section.

GOOD OBJECT/
BAD OBJECT

'Kiss Me Deadly' by Mickey Spillane (1953)

At the end of this thriller novel a woman who goes under the name of Lily Carver is holding the hero, Mike Hammer, at gunpoint. Wearing only a light bathrobe having just had an alcohol bath, she tells him how she has deceived him with another man. She is going to kill him and he is about to light a last cigarette. She reminds him that he loved her and tells him to kiss her:

Her fingers slipped through the belt of the robe, opened it. Her hands parted it slowly . . . until I could see what she was really like. I wanted to vomit worse than before. I wanted to let my guts come up and felt my belly retching.

She was a horrible caricature of a human! There was no skin, just a disgusting mass of twisted, puckered flesh from her knees to her neck making a picture of gruesome freakishness that made you want to shut your eyes against it.

The cigarette almost fell out of my mouth. The lighter shook in my hand, but I got it open.

'Fire did it, Mike. Do you think I'm pretty now?'

She laughed and I heard the insanity in it. The gun pressed into my belt as she kneeled forward, bringing the revulsion with her. 'You're going to die now . . . but first you can do it. Deadly . . . deadly . . . kiss me.'

The smile never left her mouth and before it was on me I thumped the lighter and in the moment of time before the scream blossoms into the wild cry of terror she was a mass of flame tumbling on the floor with the blue flames of alcohol turning the white of her hair into black char and her body convulsing under the agony of it. The flames were teeth that ate, ripping and tearing, into scars of other flames and her voice the shrill sound of death on the loose.

I looked, looked away. The door was closed and maybe I had enough left to make it.

THE END

The thrillers of Mickey Spillane and his private eye hero, Mike
Hammer, were widely published as pulp fiction in the 1950s and
are still in print. With some modifications, *Kiss Me Deadly* was
made into a grisly black and white movie in 1955, directed by
Robert Aldrich. In 1960 Hitchcock's film *Psycho* set a new extreme
in portraying the violent murder of a woman by a man when the
character played by Janet Leigh is knifed to death in the notorious
shower sequence. Since then both film and television have increasingly shown scenes in which women are the victims of male
aggression. There are many other examples of so-called 'slash'
movies besides the *Halloween* series, *Friday the Thirteenth* and
Dressed to Kill.

What can begin to explain the description of Gothic horror that
closes Spillane's novel? Psychoanalysis can find two ideas very
close to the surface of this fantasy. One is that feminine sexuality is
seen as posing the threat of castration. The body of the significantly
named 'Lily Carver' is imagined as mutilated 'from her knees to
her neck'. The second idea is deemed to follow immediately from
the first. Mike Hammer tries to destroy the threat by destroying
the woman. Her body is fantasized as jaws that would bite him
unless the flames of his phallic lighter can become 'teeth that ate'
her and her scars. So he meets fire with fire. In a familiar
mechanism, the fear of castration is projected back on to what
seems to cause it. The feminine as good object becomes a bad
object for him, unleashing the death drive.

But the question must be posed as to why the masculine comes
to see the feminine as castrated in the first place. It is a question

Freud tries to answer by considering the widespread importance attached to women's virginity, and it is an answer that comes close to the heart of the masculine myth. Later, I will say why I think his answer is wrong.

The account starts by noting that the insistence that a bride should be a virgin is a form of what Freud calls 'sexual bondage'. It is part of the way patriarchy treats women as dependent upon men. Patriarchy copes with the problem of incest by exchanging women in marriage. The value of that exchange is increased if women are denied sexual intercourse before marriage.

Value has been set on female virginity by Christian culture, and in bourgeois culture such virginity takes on the even greater value of a commodity. However, the evidence of anthropology is that primitive people have a quite different attitude. For them the taking of a woman's virginity is a significant act, often reserved only for a specially important man, a priest or chief. Traces of this custom are retained in Western culture. In Roman marriage a young wife was required to sit on the gigantic stone phallus of the god Priapus. And in the feudal period the lord of the manor was frequently required to take a bride's virginity according to the 'law of the first night', *jus primae noctis*.

Among primitive people it is not simply rites over virginity that set women apart from men. Menstruation also is regarded as taboo, and so is childbirth. It is not simply the first act of sexual intercourse with a woman which is taboo for men but sexual intercourse in general. Freud adds, 'one might also say that women are altogether taboo.' Noting that primitive man sets up a taboo where he fears danger, Freud goes on to suggest that a dread of woman, what he elsewhere calls *horror feminae*, 'is based on the fact that woman is different from man.' Such a feeling is not confined to primitive people but is 'still alive' in modern culture. For this the end of *Kiss Me Deadly* is more than sufficient evidence.

The Phallic System and Woman as Different

Freud offers to explain man's dread of woman by saying she wishes to castrate him. In the case of virginity, for example, the young husband fears the loss of the phallus because the bride might wish to castrate him and keep it for herself. So, in the story of Judith and Holofernes from the Apocrypha in the Old Testament, Judith seduces Holofernes, an enemy general, and then cuts off his head.

This explanation must be inadequate or simply wrong. Having analysed patriarchal attitudes at their deepest level, it then merely repeats these assumptions as though they were an explanation. Having recognized that man's dread of woman comes from the view 'that woman is different from man' it goes on to repeat that view by saying woman wants to castrate man and have the phallus. It does not say why women should want the phallus in the first place. Nor does it say why men should think women are different *from them*. Nor does it say why men should imagine women as lacking the phallus.

In human culture both the masculine and feminine individual must give up the figure of the mother because of a threat symbolized as a threat to the genitals as source of desire. Under patriarchy both the threat and the desire are imagined in terms of the phallus, the male symbol. In this myth masculinity sees itself as universal and normal. The difference between the sexes is regarded as feminine departure from a masculine norm. A phallus is attributed to the feminine so that masculinity can then find it missing and experience a threat to itself. This, the phallic system and supposed universality of the phallus, is a much better explanation of *horror feminae*.

In the dominant version masculinity is a myth not because it is not real. In fact, as the examples of popular culture have shown, its reality saturates modern culture. It is a myth in the sense that it is a wish for what is impossible, that masculinity should be like air, everywhere and the same all the way through. This is precisely what Adam wishes for in Milton's poem, that God the Father had found some way to generate mankind without the feminine and without sexual difference. In order to perpetuate itself the myth must deal somehow with what is other than masculine. It tries to banish the feminine within the male individual by denying homosexual desire. But as many instances have proved, neither repression nor sublimation can cope with the way each individual contains differences inside himself. Desire for the same sex keeps coming back.

As represented by women, the feminine outside the individual cannot be denied but can be subordinated through the exchange of women and the other tactics discussed. But throughout, the phallic system tries to assert 'woman is different from man', and that the difference lies in her non-possession of the phallus. Fetishism imagines woman with the phallus and then finds a substitute for what is missing. Her lack of the phallus is recognized as a fact, his as the threat of a possibility. In the love relation she must be seen as the phallus so that he can have the phallus in her. The phallus itself can never be more than a symbol nor castration more than a fear imposed in the name of the father. But though only a name, it is made in the father's name, not in that of someone or something else.

A single strategy underlies these varying tactics. The castration complex is an idea or meaning that arises in the gap *between* the two sexes, as the negative in which masculine is not feminine and feminine not masculine. The masculine myth aims to reconstruct castration on its own grounds. It tries to read sexual difference as her difference from him.

The myth is therefore all set to trigger aggression from the tightly bound masculine ego. Narcissism and desire are deeply interwoven. If the feminine is viewed as more deeply castrated, more lacking than masculinity, then the idea of woman appears as inherently threatening to the masculine ego. The object of desire will become an object of dread able to undo the unity of the 'I'. And the risk here is that a fearful aggression will be released against the idea of woman, as it is in the passage from Mickey Spillane. There will be the 'sound of death on the loose'.

THE MASCULINE MYTH

> *Mrs Ramsay . . . seemed to raise herself with*
> *an effort, and at once to pour erect into*
> *the air a rain of energy, a column of spray,*
> *looking at the same time animated and alive as*
> *if all her energies were being fused into force,*
> *burning and illuminating . . .*
>
> Virginia Woolf, *To the Lighthouse* (1927)

In films, television programmes, advertising, newspapers, popular songs and novels, in narratives and images that press in from every side, men are invited to recognize themselves in the masculine myth. The myth posits masculinity as natural, normal and universal. In fact it embodies a particular definition of masculinity with its own particular structure, as these various short essays have tried to show. Masculinity aims to be one substance all the way through. In order to do this it must control what threatens it both from within and without. Within, femininity and male homosexual desire must be denied; without, women and the feminine must be subordinated and held in place.

In terms of the myth masculinity wants to present itself as an essence – fixed, self-consistent, pure. In fact it has no essence and no central core. Gender is marked in three areas or levels of human experience – that of the body and the biological; that of social roles; and that at which gender is defined internally in the unconscious. The myth aims to bring together all three levels in a perfect unity, the completely masculine individual.

But it can never work like this because the levels are distinct and never simply overlap. If we use the terms 'male' for the body, 'man' for the social identity, and 'masculine' for the internal, subjective tendency, then we can see that they will not fit together evenly to make up 'one' individual. There are essentially two reasons for this. One is that each term can only fully be defined by its opposite – male/female, man/woman, masculine/feminine. And the other is that the body always has to be installed in its social roles (this is what growing up involves) by means of an internal, subjective process. And this process, which psychoanalysis describes as unconscious, always calls into play both masculine and feminine desire inside the individual.

Because gender can have no single, fixed definition, some writers have argued that it can have no fixity at all. This is an impossible dream, for it seeks to restore a kind of state of nature, like that of the infant who is, in Freud's phrase, 'polymorphously perverse', seeking pleasure everywhere without inhibition. It is in fact a state in which the infant's wishes focus mainly on the figure of the mother. And the law of human culture decrees that the mother must be given up so that the infant can take on identity as a child, able to speak coherently from its own distinct position as an 'I', desiring a person other than the mother. There can be no identity unless the object of desire is relatively defined – masculine desire for a female figure, feminine desire for a male figure. But both forms of desire are laminated together in any individual so that neither – heterosexual desire nor homosexual desire – can ever be more than a *preference*. The masculine myth insists that this preference should be heterosexual and only heterosexual. And it further demands that it should not in fact be a preference at all but rather a fixed, categorical desire for one sex *instead* of another. A man must be male and masculine and nothing else.

Clearly men do not passively live out the masculine myth imposed by the stories and images of the dominant culture. But neither can they live completely outside the myth, since it pervades the culture. Its coercive power is active everywhere – not just on screens, hoardings and paper, but inside our own heads.

Yet in whichever direction we now look this version of masculinity is in crisis, and has been for some time. The masculine myth has always tried to perpetuate its power by feigning invisibility. As soon as masculinity can be seen *as* masculinity, its power is challenged, it is called into question – for example, by any film which draws attention to how masculine the hero is. The prevalence of these has been increasing over the past ten years – calm, untroubled assurance has given way to hysterical assertion. Once upon a time, in the old Westerns of the 1950s, Gary Cooper or Randolph Scott steadfastly got on with doing what a man had to do. Now Dirty Harry leans over his victims and boasts that he has the most powerful handgun in the world.

The masculine myth is also threatened by the very existence of a book such as this, which attempts to define it. Most of the effort here has been devoted to tracking the various manoeuvres the myth adopts to keep itself alive, and the strategies it uses to keep itself concealed. That was the main purpose. But some brief, if hesitant, attempt must now be made to suggest how this new understanding might be applied. This will also provide a chance to distinguish some different layers of time and development so far elided in analysing the myth.

Possible Change

The masculine myth keeps alive in the present the thought of many dead generations. This was vividly demonstrated in the previous section with its discussion of *Kiss Me Deadly* and male fears of women.

Its roots deep and ancient, patriarchy itself forms the oldest layer in the myth; a second historical stratum that has kept re-surfacing is that of the capitalist epoch and the forms of post-Renaissance culture; and a third layer is the immediately contemporary, the way the myth is presented in popular culture today. The possibility of change applies to each of these in rather different ways.

The cultural domination of the myth in the present, through various forms of mechanical reproduction – novels, films, television, advertising, pop records – is the most amenable to change if change is what we want. Almost all the examples discussed were produced by private capital as marketable commodities. Exceptions are Michelangelo's *David* and Da Vinci's castle, which were designed for city authorities; the picture of Jesus, commissioned by the Church; and *Dynasty*, made in America by a private corporation although it is broadcast in Britain by the BBC, a state institution. Every other text is an example of something that was made to be sold.

In principle, it should be easy for a democratic society to exercise control over all these narratives and images which at present are left to the discretion of private enterprise and the demands of the market-place. In Nicaragua since the revolution, for example, the government has decreed that erotic images of women, or bits of women, should not be used in advertising. But in practice – as Geoff Hodgson has shown with great thoroughness in his recent book *The Democratic Economy* – the only existing alternative to the private control of cultural forms is their control by the state. At worst this entails the danger of totalitarianism, and at best the risk of bureaucratic puritanism. This issue leads on to another, more directly political question: how can the state become a more genuine expression of democracy and the will of the people?

The inadequacies of state control are illustrated by the following story, one which almost has the qualities of a parable. In China the People's Republic has attempted to change the social status of those who do the worst kinds of work. In consequence, in 1981 the state-controlled media put out a popular song which had the chorus line, 'How it gladdens my heart to hear the night-soil collectors coming down the mountain.' This rose to number one in the hit parade; however, it did so not because people liked the words but because they liked the melody. The moral seems to be that state control only really works if it corresponds to what people want.

The present shaping of the masculine myth is determined also at a secondary, deeper level of history, that of the capitalist era. This has fortified and intensified the myth in a number of ways. Since the early nineteenth century especially it has effected an unprecedented separation between work and home, between the sphere of production and the sphere of consumption. In doing so it has confirmed the polarization of gender by associating work with masculinity and the home with femininity. In a movement of compensation, women and the home became more idealized as work in industry became an increasingly boring routine. Here again, I think, the possibility of changing things turns into a political question related to the achievement of radical social change.

The End of Patriarchy?

Patriarchy is the oldest layer in the masculine myth and therefore the one most resistant to change. Yet patriarchy and the phallic system are always changing, as they must do, for they are not part of nature but part of human culture.

At every point this system turns on what is seen as the male symbol. Sexual difference is represented by having or not having the phallus; loss of the mother and castration are represented as a threat to the phallus; the source of the threatened castration is represented by him who bears the phallus and the name of the father. But the phallus, however deeply wrought by the traditions of patriarchal culture, is nevertheless merely a symbol. If the father is only a name, there is no reason in nature why another name might not serve as well.

The law of human culture requires that the closed circle of the infant's love for its mother must be broken if the child is to grow up and take its place in organized society. Under the patriarchal system, incest is prohibited in the name of the father. But, as Juliet Mitchell explains (in her Introduction to Lacan's essays on *Feminine Sexuality*), the problem could be solved another way:

> To date, the father stands in the position of the third term that *must* break the asocial dyadic unit of mother and child. We can see that this third term will always need to be represented by something or someone.

'Something or someone'. The function performed by the phallus is necessary if there is to be human culture, but the phallus does not have to be a 'male symbol'.

The phallus is by nature empty, a sham, for it is merely a symbol or signifier which marks sexual difference. To emphasize this, Samuel Weber's book on Freud refers to it as the 'thallus' rather than the phallus. But this inherently arbitrary symbol has taken on meaning and value from the conventions of patriarchal culture and patriarchal society. Thus it has become a *male* symbol. This is the aspect of the phallus to which Lacan draws attention when he writes of it as 'the privileged signifier' of sexual difference. A symbol or signifier cannot be privileged in itself any more than the sound of one word can be better than the sound of another, but the phallus *is* privileged in patriarchal culture, with the result that it has become a male symbol.

Perhaps here as so often poets and novelists have anticipated questions and answers that only become generally understood much later. For example, Virginia Woolf's novel of 1927, *To the Lighthouse*, takes the lighthouse of its title and narrative as a phallic symbol. Throughout the story the male members of Mrs Ramsay's family keep trying to reach the lighthouse, although when they do finally sail to it their quest has rather lost its point. Yet in other passages in the novel the image of the erect beacon takes on quite different meanings, especially when it and its light are associated with Mrs Ramsay. The passage quoted at the top of this section is a good instance. It suggests how the shape of the lighthouse is still visible but is now substantiated by something else, by a column of water linked closely with the figure of the mother, Mrs Ramsay. It is not, I think, either fanciful or an exaggeration to regard the lighthouse in the novel as being a phallus without masculine qualities, a dephallicized phallus, a possible third term to break the relation of mother and child, but one which does not belong clearly either to the father or the mother.

If a new unisex or ungendered definition of the third term came into existence it would save men from the impossible burden of trying to perpetuate the phallic system. It is not easy to foresee all the consequences of such a cultural revolution. From many possibilities I shall choose one line of speculation to pursue here, because it highlights something important that kept emerging in the discussion of the masculine idealization of women. We might now think briefly of how a new definition of the third term might affect the relation between fathers and sons.

In a number of places, this analysis of masculinity has drawn on the contrast between the development of heterosexual desire in male and female. Both little boys and little girls begin by loving the figure of the mother. While girls transfer their feeling from the mother to the father and then to the bridegroom, boys transfer from the mother to the bride. This psychoanalytic account has been used to explain a masculine tendency to idealize women as The Woman. The double standard corresponds to mother versus other women, and being in love imports a crippling tendency to idealize into the sexual relation.

So far the proximity of mother and bride for men has been accepted as though it were an unchanging aspect of human experience. It may not be so. In order to move from the mother to the bride the little boy must, at present, challenge the father for possession of the mother. He must challenge the father because patriarchy works in the name of the father. But if, as Juliet Mitchell suggests, the necessary break from the mother could be signalled by something else, a third term which did not entail the father and a male symbol, the situation might be changed. Under the presently dominant system the little boy must give up his homosexual desire for the father so as to contest possession of the mother. If the system were no longer patriarchal he would not have to do this. The figure of the father could be retained for a while as an object of desire, and this would interpose a figure *between* the mother and the bride. If the little boy's trajectory moved from the mother to the father to the bride, the latter would be much less susceptible to being idealized. The damaging effect of seeing a woman as The Woman might be diminished or even disappear entirely. But how could the third term forbidding the child's first incestuous love for the mother come to have a non-phallic, non-masculine meaning and value?

Let us take the risk of imagining the future. Utopianism should not, after all, be left to science fiction. Though it can be an escape from the present it can also be a way of confronting the present, to see what needs to be changed here and now. We must assume that the human race will resist the seductions of the death drive as represented by 30,000 warheads. We ought to be able to think what society would be like in, say, the year 2411.

To empty the phallus of its privilege as a *male* symbol will almost certainly require the dismantling of patriarchal culture itself. Although in itself a mere symbol – a signifier that could be replaced by 'thallus' as Weber has suggested – the phallus acquires force and value from the conventions of patriarchal culture (in fact considerable organization would be needed even to get all English speakers to use the term 'thallus' regularly instead of 'phallus'). And patriarchal culture corresponds to the structures and institutions of the patriarchal society through which it is reproduced.

To make the new third term, the new signifier of sexual difference, into a real symbol, active at the deepest levels of the unconscious, would presuppose wholly new forms of human culture. Sexual relations must be remade, and so must the institutionalized forms of marriage and family life, possibly through the development of more widely dispersed and looser forms of kinship groupings, groups perhaps based on something more than friendship and less than blood relationship. But the implications carry further. As was suggested in the earlier sections on 'The Masculine Ego', and particularly in 'Man and Nation', patriarchy finds a forceful and aggressive expression in the idea of the nation state. It is hard to foresee the end of patriarchy before the nation state has been absorbed by some form of genuine world government. Possibly then the function of the third term, whose threat denies the mother to the human infant, might be performed by a symbolic representation of 'The United Nations'. Even to speculate along these lines makes clear the scale of change that will have to occur. But by 2411 all this might have been achieved.

List of Texts

All the texts by Freud are in the Penguin Freud Library (PFL). Those by Jacques Lacan are: *Écrits*, Tavistock, 1977; *The Four Fundamental Concepts of Psychoanalysis*, Penguin, 1980; *Feminine Sexuality*, Macmillan, 1982.

Introduction
The Ego and the Id, especially section III, PFL 11.

The Mysterious Phallus
Group Psychology and the Analysis of the Ego, especially chapter vi, PFL 12; 'Some Neurotic Mechanisms in Jealousy, Paranoia and Homosexuality', PFL 10; '"Civilized" Sexual Morality and Modern Nervous Illness', PFL 12.

Fathers and Sons
Introductory Lectures, lecture 21, PFL 1; 'The Dissolution of the Oedipus Complex', PFL 7;
Totem and Taboo, PFL 13.

The Castle of the Self
Leonardo da Vinci and a Memory of his Childhood, PFL 14; 'Inhibitions, Symptoms and Anxiety', PFL 10;
'The Mirror Stage' and 'Aggressivity in Psychoanalysis', both in *Écrits*.

The Male Body
Introductory Lectures, lecture 26, PFL 1.

Men at War
The Ego and the Id, especially section V, PFL 11;
'Some Psychical Consequences of the Anatomical Distinction between the Sexes', PFL 7;
'Creative Writers and Daydreaming', PFL 14.
Beyond the Pleasure Principle, PFL 11.

The Magic Keg of Beer
Three Essays on the Theory of Sexuality, PFL 7;
Civilization and its Discontents, especially section II, PFL 12.

Masculine Style (1): Clarity
'Fetishism', PFL 7;
'The Agency of the Letter in the Unconscious', *Écrits*.

Masculine Style (3): Obscenity
'On Transformations of Instinct as Exemplified in Anal Eroticism', PFL 7;
'Character and Anal Eroticism', PFL 7.

The Same Sex
'Hysterical Phantasies and their relation to Bisexuality', PFL 10;
'Psychoanalytic Notes on an Autobiographical Account of a Case of Paranoia (Dementia Paranoides)', PFL 9.

Exchanging Women (1): Marriage
'The Dissolution of the Oedipus Complex', PFL 7;
'The Signification of the Phallus', *Écrits*.

Exchanging Women (2): Jokes
Jokes and their Relation to the Unconscious, especially section III, PFL 6.

The Madonna and the Whore
'A Special Type of Choice of Object Made by Men (Contributions to the Psychology of Love, I)', PFL 7;
'On the Universal Tendency to Debasement in the Sphere of Love' (Contributions to the Psychology of Love, II)', PFL 7.

The Idea of The Woman
'God and the *Jouissance* of The Woman. A Love Letter', *Feminine Sexuality*.

Being in Love
'Mourning and Melancholia', PFL 11;

Group Psychology and the Analysis of the Ego, especially section VIII, PFL 12;

'Of the Gaze as *Objet Petit a*', *The Four Fundamental Concepts of Psychoanalysis*;

'A Love Letter', *Feminine Sexuality*.

Fame, Wealth, and the Love of Women
Introductory Lectures, lecture 23, PFL 1.

Jealousy
'Some Neurotic Mechanisms in Jealousy, Paranoia and Homosexuality', PFL 10.

Good Object/Bad Object
'The Taboo of Virginity (Contributions to the Psychology of Love III)', PFL 7.

FURTHER READING

Psychoanalysis
Mitchell, J., *Psychoanalysis and Feminism*, Penguin, 1975
Weber, S., *The Legend of Freud*, University of Minnesota, 1982

The History of Sexuality
Foucault, M., *The History of Sexuality*, Penguin, 1981
Heath, S., *The Sexual Fix*, Macmillan, 1982
Hirst, P. & Woolley, P., *Social Relations and Human Attributes*, Tavistock, 1982
Nicholson, J., *Men and Women: How Different Are They?*, OUP, 1984
Weeks, J., *Sex, Politics and Society*, Longman, 1981
Weeks, J., *Sexuality and its Discontents*, Routledge & Kegan Paul, 1985

Sociology
Pleck, J. H., *The Myth of Masculinity*, MIT, 1981
Pleck, J. H. & Sawyer, J., *Men and Masculinity*, Prentice-Hall, 1974
Stearns, P. N., *Be a Man*, Holmes and Meir, 1979
Tolson, A., *The Limits of Masculinity*, Tavistock, 1977

Masculinity
Coveney, L. *et al.*, *The Sexuality Papers*, Hutchinson, 1984
Dollimore, J., 'Masculinity and Homophobia', in *Literature Teaching Politics*, Bristol Polytechnic, 1985
Ehrenreich, B., *The Hearts of Men*, Pluto, 1983
Hocquenghem, G., *Homosexual Desire*, Allison & Busby, 1978
Ingham, M., *The Male Myth Exposed*, Century, 1984

Metcalf, A. & Humphries, M. (eds), *The Sexuality of Men*, Pluto, 1985

Phillips, E. (ed.), *The Left and the Erotic*, Lawrence & Wishart, 1983

Taylor, H. (ed.), *Literature Teaching Politics 1985*, Bristol Polytechnic, 1985

Literature

Belsey, C., *Critical Practice*, Methuen, 1980
Fiedler, L. A., *Love and Death in the American Novel*, Paladin, 1970
Schwenger, P., *Phallic Critiques*, Routledge & Kegan Paul, 1984
Sedgwick, E. K., *Between Men*, Columbia University Press, 1985

Film

Bennett, T. & Woollacott, J., *Bond and Beyond*, Macmillan, 1986
Ellis, J., *Visible Fictions*, Routledge & Kegan Paul, 1982
Heath, S., *Questions of Cinema*, Macmillan, 1981
Lapsley, R. & Westlake, M., *Thinking about Cinema*, Manchester University Press, 1986

Television

Bennett, T. *et al.* (ed), *Popular Television and Film*, BFI/Open University, 1981
Fiske, J. & Hartley, J., *Reading Television*, Methuen, 1978
Masterman, L. (ed.), *Television Mythologies*, Comedia, 1984

Images

Barthes, R., *Mythologies*, Paladin, 1973
Berger, J., *Ways of Seeing*, Penguin, 1972
Bryson, N., *Vision and Painting*, Macmillan, 1983
Walters, M., *The Nude Male*, Penguin, 1979
Williamson, J., *Decoding Advertisements*, Boyars, 1978